POPE PIUS XII LIBRARY, ST. JOSEPH COL.

3 2528 07056 9340

Wide Ruins

D1562911

WIDE

Memories from

Published in cooperation with the Albuquerque Museum

RUINS

a Navajo Trading Post

Sallie Wagner

FOREWORD BY
Edward T. Hall

University of New Mexico Press
ALBUQUERQUE

© 1997 by Sallie Wagner. All rights reserved
First Edition

Library of Congress Cataloging-in-Publication Data

Wagner, Sallie R.
Wide ruins / Sallie Wagner; foreword by Edward T. Hall—1st ed.
p.   cm.
ISBN 0-8263-1805-3 (pbk.)
1. Navajo Indians—Social life and customs.   2. Navajo Indian
Reservation.   3. Wagner, Sallie R.   4. Indian traders—Navajo
Indian Reservation—Biography.   I. Title.
E99.N3W24   1997
9.1′35004972—dc21   96-45821
                                                              CIP

Contents

To the Navajos of Wide Ruins.

To Mildy Hall whose encouraging interest and helpful suggestions persuaded me to write down the tales I had been telling. I am saddened that she is not here to read this book.

To M. H. and Arnie Rivin for their encouraging interest.

To Bill LeBlond for his help in some of the business details.

To Nanci Mon who cheerfully suffered through my terrible typing to interpret it on her computer.

My heartfelt thanks to all.

Foreword

Edward T. Hall

It was the period when visiting Navajo and Hopi reservations became fashionable. *Wide Ruins* is the record of a young couple, Sallie and Bill Lippincott—newlyweds, well educated and goodwilled—who experienced the pull of the country and the people and wondered how they could possibly find a way to anchor themselves to that magic land. Because they adopted neither the attitudes nor the manners of the old-time traders, the Lippincotts became favorites among white visitors to the Navajo Reservation. Newcomers themselves, as well as literate and outgoing, they were the ideal people to tell the outside world the story of trading with the Navajos.

Although Sallie and Bill didn't know it at the time, the 1930s were a period during which every aspect of Navajo life would be altered. John Collier, the new commissioner of Indian Affairs, had just introduced drastic changes by modeling Navajo government after our own. In addition the Soil Conservation Service, in the name of preservation of the land, introduced and enforced reductions in Navajo herds of sheep, goats, horses, and cattle, leaving an indelible mark on that most depressed of all economies. It was this desperate marginal environment that the Lippincotts stepped into when they bought the defunct trading post at Wide Ruins—an Anasazi site on an unimproved road between Chambers, Arizona and the new Navajo Reservation headquarters at Window Rock.

Virtually without exception, when people think of the Navajo country of the thirties they carry images in their heads based on books and stories which are for the most part modified to conform to our stereotypes of the Indians and the country in which they lived. In contrast to such stereotypes, this modest little volume offers an unvarnished account of a time, a people, and a country that no longer exist. To her credit, the author has done her best to avoid the temptation to embellish a story that will be one of the last to be written about firsthand experiences prior to the time when the twentieth century placed its stamp on the Navajo people.

In those days, in the central part of the reservation, Navajos owned horses, Studebaker wagons, and one automobile—a Model T Ford with no top that belonged to one of my foremen, a wonderful man whose name translated "The Tall Man Who Stutters." In the part of the reservation where I supervised a dozen crews building earth dams to preserve a small fraction of the runoff when it rained, only four out of perhaps eight to ten thousand Navajos spoke English. It is safe to say that for all intents and purposes, one lived in an all-Navajo world. Only bits and pieces of vocabulary referred to white culture: nakiyahl meant two bits, from the Spanish pieces of eight; chidi (as in city with a t) meant automobile; toh (toe said forcibly) meant water, and chidi toh meant gasoline, which ran the noisy, rattling, not-so-dependable vehicles that were always getting stuck, driven by bilekaahna (white men). In fact there were parts of the reservation where there were people who had never seen a white man—though this was not the case, of course, in the Wide Ruins area.

Both the people and the country had a low tolerance for newcomers and slow learners, which Sallie Wagner illustrates in stunning detail when she writes about Easterners trying to reach faraway places like Chinle. Getting around in those days was not only a challenge but an education. There were no roads as we know them and no bridges across the arroyos (dry washes). During my time on the Hopi Reservation when it rained on Black Mesa, to the north, it was not unusual to have to sit on the edge of the wash until the water went down a day or so later. Some overanxious innocents would try to cross these washes before the water had stopped running—a mistake which could result in the loss of an automobile or even a life.

As I write this, I find my mind jumping to Africa and the Australian outback and how the local people are pictured in the adventure movies made about them and their country: primitive, because they didn't have the things that we have, didn't dress the way we do, didn't speak English, and had no roads. Then my mind jumps back to the Navajo Reservation in the thirties and forties. In spite of our primitive system for getting around, there was something so natural and right about the way the Navajos lived (when evaluated in their terms, not ours), taking each change in their stride, that it used to shock those of us who had become a part of the country when we heard Easterners putting that same country and its people down because of the lack of indoor plumbing in the Navajo hogans. There was no such thing as incongruity. You could walk into a trading post and hear one of the clerks call to another, "Charge that flour to Many Beads' Wife Number 4; she only has five dollars on her credit, by the way." Polygyny was a way of life and as natural to the people as eating and breathing.

What makes Sallie Wagner's story come alive is its simplicity, its honesty, and its lack of cant. Generous and full of goodwill, she and her husband showed the Navajo women how to produce high-quality wool to be woven into rugs using local vegetal dyes in low-key colors, and they underwrote the project with their own money. This effort eventually put thousands of dollars into the weavers' pockets.

Almost without exception, those of us who worked and lived with "the people," or the diné—the Navajos' name for themselves—are grateful for the privilege of having been with them before they were subjected to the mill of the white man's culture. This story is a must read for those interested in the Navajo people in the early days. Sallie Wagner has managed to catch and retain the essence of what it meant to be white in a Navajo world that was unbelievably different.

ONE

A Business unto Itself

We slipped sideways into the Navajo Indian trading post business. Most of the traders who deal with Indians (and not with tourists) have grown up on reservations. They are the sons and daughters of parents whose lives have been dedicated to dealing with Indians in one capacity or another, as missionaries, government employees, or merchants.

We had no experience as traders but we did have a nodding acquaintance with cultures other than our own. We met in 1936, in the Anthropology Department at the University of Chicago, where I was working for my bachelor's degree and Bill for his master's. He had already graduated from the University of California, where his father had been a professor. My interest in anthropology grew out of a romantic interest in Indians. As my home in West Virginia was on a prehistoric campsite, I found many stone tools in the gardens and corn fields around me.

Cozy and Inja

Newly married in 1938, we had come to the Navajo Reservation for Bill to take a ranger job at Canyon de Chelly. Here we became friends with old-time trader Cozy McSparron and his wife, Inja. Cozy insisted that she was named for her grandmother's home state—Inja Anna.

Like us, Cozy was an exception to the usual biography of the trader. As a lightweight boxer he had come to Gallup for an exhibition of his prowess. At that time there were two traders at Chinle, a town of a few buildings at the mouth of Canyon de Chelly in northeastern Arizona. The two traders were at odds with one another, sometimes at serious odds. One of them hired Cozy to come out to the Navajo Reservation and teach him to fight. Every morning, in sparring, the trader was knocked out. At the end of the winter he still had not learned to fight, but Cozy had learned the trading business.

He stayed on at the Chinle post, eventually buying the place for himself.

When we left the Park Service in 1938 and were at loose ends, Cozy jokingly suggested we buy a trading post. We mulled it over. The suggestion didn't seem such a joke after all, and the next thing we knew, Cozy had unearthed three possibilities: Wide Ruins, Nazlini, and Sawmill, all on the reservation. The last two were too close to Cozy, and we did not want to get into competition with him. So we chose Wide Ruins, eighty miles south of Cozy's post. After a crash course in trading as practiced by the McSparrons, we moved into Wide Ruins. The few years we spent there were the best of our lives.

With the Defiance Plateau to the east and the Painted Desert to the west, the community of Wide Ruins consisted of the trading post, a day school on a hill a mile away, and a range rider's shack by the arroyo between. The store was in the middle of an Anasazi ruin, built several hundred years ago around a lively spring.

Wide Ruins, spring

Wide Ruins, winter. Photo by Bill Lippincott

The school was staffed by one teacher, an assistant teacher (who informed me that she "learned the Navajos to speak English"), and a driver for the bus that daily traversed roads that were often only wagon tracks. The one-room igloo-shaped hogans where the Navajos lived were set back in the hills and in the desert in a radius of fifteen miles from the post. There were no communities of buildings; Navajo hogans are isolated homes. During the winters, which are long in northern Arizona, the temperature is often below zero. When there was snow or rain, or in the spring when the dry winds blew and sand piled up, the roads, such as they were, were all but impassable. The children whom the bus gathered up were not the slicked-down, book-toting, bundled-up children that Anglo school buses transport. The Navajo children were undisciplined little kids, usually hungry and unwashed. When they got to school they had to be fed, warmed, cleaned, and organized. And this had to be done every day. Teachers on the reservation were dedicated individuals.

The Bureau of Indian Affairs range rider lived in a shack by the arroyo. He was responsible for the physical aspect of the area. By horseback or truck he kept track of the wells, the windmills, and the small control dams scattered around the countryside. He also was in charge of the yearly dipping of the sheep and branding of the horses and cattle, which always took place in the store corrals.

Sheep dipping was a time of great bustle and excitement. The many flocks drifted in from all directions. The deep concrete trough between two sections of the corrals was filled with an antiseptic solution of water and nicotine. One by one the sheep were tossed into the trough and guided through it by women wielding forked sticks. In the receiving pen the sheep could be counted to make sure that the owners had not exceeded their varied allotments, which depended on local conditions. Allotments were necessary to prohibit overgrazing.

Dipping sheep

The years before World War II were hard ones for Navajo people. The livestock reduction program that left such psychological and social scarring on them was coming to a close. In 1868, after the Navajo Wars, when the Navajos were returned to what was to be their reservation, the United States government supplied each Indian with a small number of sheep. But the people had been such good stockmen since then that the herds had increased far beyond the carrying capacity of the desert range. So the Bureau of Indian Affairs devised a program to dispose of surplus horses, cattle, goats, and sheep. The Navajo Tribal Council itself, under the wise leadership of Chairman Henry Chee Dodge, voted approval, and the program was put into operation by the federal government.

The first night we spent in our new home, a herd of horses en route to the railroad was bivouacked in our corral, and two or three

Water trough with sheep, goats, and horses

Reconstruction

of them, too weak to go on, were shot. In spite of such sad episodes, and drastic and misunderstood as it was, the stock reduction program was absolutely necessary to save what little range remained. It was a necessary step, but it left the tribe with little source of livelihood.

The Wide Ruins Navajos were desperately in need of economic help. We were in need of workmen to restore the buildings. So we hired all the good workers we could find, and we became instantly important to the area.

Perhaps the best help that Cozy McSparron gave us was the suggestion that we hire Bill Cousins, who had worked for him in the past. He was to be only temporary, until we learned the details of trading, but he proved invaluable and stayed on all the years that we were on the reservation. He was the son of a trader and spoke Navajo, as did his wife, Jean. In the thirteen years we were there, doing business on unsecured credit, we lost only about four hundred dollars,

Walter Ashley, one of the workers we hired to restore the trading post

thanks to Bill Cousin's expertise and the honesty of the Wide Ruins Navajos.

Indian trading is a business unto itself, so Cozy's educational course was necessary. For years we hoped that the IRS would choose us to investigate, but they never did. We gloated over the vision of a frazzled investigator poring over our books trying to trace a transaction from Indian to trading post to wholesale house to trading post and back to an Indian again without involving any monetary exchange.

It took some months for the people to decide that it might be all right to trade with us. The test came when Bent Knee arrived to take a deerskin out of pawn and found that the skin was still in the building. It was the custom, when selling a post, to also sell off all the things that were in pawn, thus clearing still-owed debts. But we had bought all the pawned goods at the price for which they were pawned, and Bent Knee was overjoyed to find that his belongings and those of all the other customers were still available for redemption. This event, of course, was not a complete breakthrough but it did bore a hole in the "buckskin curtain" that would be widened over the years.

The Navajo economy was based on sheep; lambs were sold in the fall and wool in the spring. At those times the bills run up by customers were paid off. We had to know the approximate size of each family's flock in order to know how much credit to allow them. We sold the lambs as feeders (animals that would be fed to increase their weight) directly to buyers who came through from stock yards in the Middle West. In the same way we sold wool to traveling buyers from the Boston wool market. In the fall we hired herders from among our steady customers, turning over to them the sheep we bought each day. At the end of a month of buying, these sheep were slowly moved to the railroad in Chambers, eighteen miles away by either land or truck, loaded into cars and sent to the Colorado feed lots.

Bent Knee

Bill Cousins buying lambs. Photo by John Adair

Hide buyers came through once in a while from Utah to buy sheep and cattle hides and any wild animal pelts we might happen to have. But that was a minor source of income. Fall sales of pinyon nuts, on the other hand, gave the Navajos an economic boost in a good year. We sold pinyons through the wholesale houses in Gallup, which sometimes bought the lambs and wool, too. That was a good way to build up credit with the wholesalers, who would furnish us with goods to trade to the Navajos, who would bring in things for us to take to the wholesalers. Round and round it went.

We kept pawn records in a separate account book. Day-to-day transactions were in a regular daybook. If an Indian were in need of money or credit and had nothing to trade he would bring in anything of value that he had and pawn it. We usually kept the pawned items for thirteen months and then put them on display for another month to alert the owners that their possessions were going dead and could be sold. But if something was of particular value to the owner, we would keep it indefinitely, as did most traders. As a matter of fact, it was the custom of Navajos all over the reservation to use the pawn rooms of posts as safety deposit boxes. Things of value were more secure locked up there than in an unguarded hogan. Traders made a practice of lending pawned articles back to their owners when there was particular need. Often at the end of the thirteen months a valued article would be redeemed and then pawned again an hour or so later. At Wide Ruins we tried to keep the loan at about half the value of the piece so that the owner could more easily redeem it. The Indians' possessions were their savings accounts and, once gone, they were gone forever. If redeemed, they were money in the bank and could be drawn upon again and again. So we had very little pawn go "dead." When pawn was redeemed no interest was charged. Stores dealing with the tourist public often stress that they have dead pawn for sale. This sounds romantic but has very little to do with the actual value of the piece. There are as many poor pieces of jewelry pawned as there are good.

It was by no means only jewelry that was brought to us as security for a loan. Saddles, baskets, store-bought tools, anything at all was stowed away in the pawn room and in the safe. We had to know the value of the article to the Navajo as well as its value in the commercial world. A deerskin, for instance, was worth more if it had a tail than if it were tailless. A deerskin with a tail is necessary for certain ceremonies, whereas a tailless one could be used only for making moccasins or for some other base purpose. We sometimes teased a customer by tying a pawn tag on a baby. One day a woman came in carrying a newborn baby strapped to the usual cradle board. She hoisted baby and board up onto the counter and I chucked the baby under its chin, made cooing noises at it and then asked the mother, "Is it a boy or a girl?" She looked at me as though I'd lost my mind and then answered shortly, "Of course!!"

The daybook, of course, referred to all ordinary post transactions. A customer would bring in something to trade and we would tell him what we would give him for it in terms of cash. We did not dicker, as we did not like to bargain, but we tried to give honest and fair prices and the Navajos almost always agreed to our offer. If the customer wanted cash we gave it to him, but he usually wanted to take it out in trade. Then we would give him a *naltsos*—a sales slip with his name and the amount due written on it. Sometimes, at the customer's request, we would have to write out a new *naltsos* after each purchase, but usually we kept a running account on the back of the slip, deducting each purchase as it was made.

Store interior. Bill Cousins, Bill and Sallie Lippincott behind counter

A sack of flour, a can of baking powder, some shortening, and, in season, a watermelon were often the first purchases made. Before World Was II a large can of tomatoes was added to that primary list, but after the war tomatoes were scratched. I still wonder why. Usually, the last nickel was spent on five caramel lollipops. If the Indian did not trade out the entire credit for what he had brought in, we would either given him cash for change or another *naltsos*, depending on which he asked for. The *naltsos* were often traded among the Indians themselves just as cash might be. They were good only at the issuing trading post. Anyone having one could take it to that post and exchange it for cash.

In the not too distant past the posts issued a form of scrip, metal discs or octagons or squares that were stamped with the name of the post and the amount that each coin was worth. My collection of these no-longer-used pieces was once on exhibit at the Northern Trust Bank in Chicago. I had an advertising brochure from the bank boasting that it had an example of every coin ever issued in the United States. I challenged that statement and sent them a box of trading post money they had never seen before.

Then there was the wool book. When we bought raw fleece wool in the spring we would sort it and keep the long staple wool to trade back to the weavers, as that kind of wool was best for hand spinning and weaving. Sometimes we would trade it outright but more often we would lend it to a weaver. Once in a while we bought wool from the western part of the reservation where there were still many long-haired, four-horned Spanish/Churro sheep. We weighed the fleece and entered the amount in the wool book. Then when a weaver to whom we had issued wool brought in the finished rug the weight had to balance out. In that way she was unable to take rugs made with our wool to another post. If it didn't balance in weight it had to balance in value—the value of the rug should exceed the value of the loaned wool.

When we finally left Wide Ruins we donated our account books to Cornell University where they can be referred to by anyone interested in the trading business.

Trading was a slow business. High-pressure salesmanship made the customers suspicious: there must be some nefarious reason why you wanted to get rid of whatever you were selling. We kept a dartboard nailed to the shelves at one end of the long counter, and hour after hour we threw darts and became quite expert at it. Sometimes, if a game were at a critical stage, we would actively discourage business transactions until we had finished. The customers never objected. They weren't in any more of a hurry than we were. Even the occasional tourist became bemused.

Sometimes I would think we were leading an escapist existence on the Navajo Reservation with no responsibilities toward the world at large. Then I remembered how the very fact of the existence of Wide Ruins seemed to mean so much to so many people. Several newspaper and magazine articles were written about our life on the reservation and Alberta Hannum wrote two books about Jimmy Toddy, a young Navajo boy who was a great friend of ours (see Chapter 9). We received many letters from men, women, and children asking questions or wanting to come work for us.

"Dear Sir," wrote one correspondent, "I have read the book about you with much pleasure. I would like to buy a few acres with an adobe cottage and drinkable water in your region. Can an individual buy real estate on an Indian Reservation or National Forest Reservation?

"Do you have utilities available in that area? Electricity, Telephone, Gas, etc? What is the lowest winter temperature? Are dust storms and floods and Spring frosts bad there? Are you able to grow anything at all? What is your elevation?

"Where can you look for the veins of turquoise that the Indians make their ornaments from? In that Western country is it possible to hire Indian women to build adobe buildings? Will they work for whites?"

Perhaps reading about this place or visiting it was like a gasp of fresh air to someone who was suffocating in the hurly-burly of modern culture. Places like Wide Ruins may actually play a vital role, existing as air holes for the rest of the world.

Once in a while, tourists would drop in, usually because they were lost and on the wrong road. The tourists would be curious and chatty, and the Navajos would be suddenly quiet and wooden-faced. As soon as the visitors left we would be treated to a burlesque performance of their behavior.

When tourists and unassimilated tribal people come together they often view each other as childlike. Tribal people don't know the subtle details of the tourists' culture. And the tourist doesn't know the subtle details of the tribal culture. Both are intrigued and curious about anything that is new to them. But when some lost tourists ask which way is north, south, east or west, or try unsuccessfully to

Photo of tourist by Joe Toddy

make conversation and ask question after question about everything around them, an Indian is sure to comment (in his own language), "they act like children."

Navajo humor was not always postponed until the tourists had left. Sometimes an unusually inquisitive or intrusive tourist would be the butt of a joke here and now. I remember Joe Toddy borrowing my camera and asking for twenty-five cents to give a snap-shooting man so Joe could take *his* picture.

There was also the time when a friend, riding in the car with me and two Navajo women, started to snap a passing wagon when she suddenly remembered my admonition about taking pictures of usually reluctant subjects. She interrupted herself and began to put her camera away until one of the back-seat passengers reassured her, "Go ahead. There aren't any Indians around here."

I have known only two Indians with no sense of humor. One was from Santo Domingo Pueblo and the other was a Wide Ruins area medicine man whom we knew as Little Jimmy. Little Jimmy once inadvertently ate a sand dollar that we had brought from a Pacific beach and left on the counter for curious customers to examine. The other Navajos in the store thought it was hilarious that the old man had mistaken the dollar for a cookie but Jimmy saw nothing funny about it at all. He grumpily demanded a sack of real cookies which I provided and then started to fill his other requests until my eyes began to cross as I looked at him. He was wearing his usual spectacles but both lenses were broken and half of each was missing, one horizontally and one vertically. The next time I went to Gallup I bought him three pairs of new glasses of varying degrees of magnification so he could take his choice.

A trading post was not all business by any means. The posts were the center of social activity, always places of interest and fun to the Navajos. Because they lived in isolated family groups, a central gathering place was very important. They tended to come to the traders for solutions to almost any problem—domestic, medical, or techni-cal. We doctored them, laid down the law about family fights, made out their work applications, and wrote their letters for them, often sending to mail order houses for things that they could have bought from us. Once old Cut Hair had us subscribe to *Esquire* for him. But when the first copy came, he was bitterly disappointed that the little manikin that served as the magazine's logo was not included.

There was always a large copper pot of coffee on the wood stove that dominated the customers' side of the high counters and there were always friends or relatives, also in for a day's trading, who were seldom seen at any other time. The free coffee, laced with a large dollop of sugar from a deep drawer watched over by the storekeeper, was one of the delights to be savored at the end of a long ride by horseback or wagon.

Some Indians came galloping in one evening to ask for help in stopping a fight that was developing between Frank Billy and John Joe Red Eye. It was a continuation of the same fight that landed Frank Billy in the hospital with a temperature of 104°, broken ribs, and a punctured lung. It had also been the cause of John Joe Red Eye's sojourn in the jug at Window Rock, the head agency. Now both men were home again and neither seemed to have forgotten his peeve. So Bill Cousins and Bill Lippincott rushed off to the rescue. I understand that my husband made a most impressive speech all filled with terms like Goodness and Evil, Unhappiness and Happiness. He said he felt so silly. But apparently it did some good because the as-sembled Indians, including the combatants, all went home, thought deeply and earnestly, and came to announce that Bill was right and that they would forget the whole thing. They wouldn't even talk about it—especially the women wouldn't talk about it.

TWO

Under the Cottonwoods

The house, the store, and the storerooms were one long building backed against the hill that was partly formed by the ruins of the prehistoric town. In front of the store and the house were tall cottonwoods. The Anasazi ruins, known to the Navajos as Kinatiela, Wide Ruined House, covered a few acres on which no pinyon or juniper trees grew.

The Anasazi were ancestors of today's Pueblo peoples. In its prehistoric heyday the Wide Ruined House was centered around a dependable spring. The ancient people had encased it in walls, forming a nine-foot cube. That spring never failed and was the best-tasting water in that section of Arizona. Other water tasted of alkali. In the distant past the spring had sustained about five hundred villagers and now, in times of drought, sustained innumerable Navajos who hauled away its water in oil drums.

Aerial view of trading post, house, and spring. Photo by Bill Lippincott

In the late 1800s, the Day brothers built the trading post. It, too, depended on that spring. So the post and living quarters were built beside the water. Spring and buildings were at the bottom of a small ravine, and the two wings of the ruins spread like butterfly wings up over the two adjacent sandy hills. The Anasazi had had views of their desert domain—the Defiance Plateau to the east and the Painted Desert to the west. But tucked into the ravine as we were, we had a limited view. Every evening at sunset my little old Scottie dog would trudge up to the topmost ruin and sit patiently staring west until the sun disappeared. We often joined him there.

When we first moved into Wide Ruins there was a lot of renovating to be done. The house had walls of stone except for one end of the long living room which was simply chicken wire covered over with plaster. There were two bedrooms and a bathroom, but the bathroom was separated from the bedrooms by the living room, the kitchen, and the laundry.

Roofs were supported by horizontal logs onto which were tacked sheets of beaverboard. The spaces between the ends of the log rafters

The house. Photo by L. Lake

Spring house

Bill Lippincott in the living room after restoration

were not filled by anything at all, so the wind and birds had free access. They took advantage of it, too.

The walls between the rooms were built of stone, just like the outer walls, and when we wired the place for electricity we had to use a star drill to make holes to run the wires through. In every room there was a fireplace, the only heat we ever used in all the years we lived there although the winters were cold indeed, often below zero. There was plenty of dead wood, which we bought from our customers, and, once lit, the fragrant fires did not go out until spring.

A small gasoline generator supplied us with feeble electric light until after several years, we installed a diesel generator which was stronger and more reliable.

All the outside walls of all the buildings were covered with cement plaster with the exception of the spring house. Up on the hill, across the arroyo, was another small unplastered building that had been the original trading post before the big one was built. That building was my husband's office until, after the war, we converted it into a studio for Jimmy Toddy, who by that time had become well known as an artist under his new name of Beatien Yazz.

A door in the kitchen opened directly into the store with the pawn safe on the left and the candy counter on the right. Both saw a great deal of activity, particularly the candy counter if there was a bountiful crop of pinyon nuts in the fall. Little children would solemnly approach the high counter, peer up expectantly, and silently hold out a handful of nuts. Such a small number of nuts would be worth practically nothing but they had been laboriously gathered one at a time. So, many lollipops were handed out in exchange, and the nuts were added to the huge burlap sacks that were the harvest of the adults who had brought in many pounds at a time. We usually sold the full sacks to the Gross Kelley wholesale house in Gallup. The nuts ultimately ended up in the Italian district of New York or else in cans of

Store interior. Bill Lippincott (center) stands in front of door to kitchen.
Photo by Bob Branstead

mixed nuts where they always sifted maddeningly to the bottom and were hard to pick up.

The refrigerator, directly across the narrow aisle from the candy counter, was filled to the brim with bottles of soda pop. Priced at a nickel a bottle, soda pop was nearly always part of a trading transaction.

A left turn brought you face to face with shelf after shelf of canned fruit, meat, and vegetables. Across the aisle was the main counter with its deep drawers of sugar, tanbark for dying moccasin leather, and odds and ends. The loose sugar was kept readily available for the cans of tomatoes which the customers wanted opened with the sweetening sprinkled on top. When canned tomatoes fell out of favor after World War II the sugar-tomato routine died out.

There were times when there would be a suspicious run on cakes of yeast and cans of peaches. Then we would relegate those commodities to the storage room until we judged that the urge to manufacture some illegal product had died out. Alcohol was not much of a problem until after World War II.

The canned food shelves ended alongside a doorway that led into the back storerooms, one of which was a display area for the rugs that had been brought in by the weavers. On the other side of that door was a small section devoted to medicines, all approved by the doctors at the Ganado hospital, twenty miles to the north. Pepto Bismol, Alka-Seltzer, and a powerful smelling rub for sore muscles were the best sellers. Next were shelves of dry goods, mostly bolts of brightly patterned percale from which the women made their voluminous skirts, and bolts of scintillating velveteen for their blouses. The favorite color of velveteen was blue. It faded badly in the sun, but it was very hard to choose a more practical color. Across the aisle a glass counter exhibited all sorts of notions, including the popular bottles of perfume which, at ten cents a bottle, smelled like vanilla and probably could have been used to flavor a cake.

As the aisle turned to the left again, it passed shelves of shoes and across from them another glass case in which pawn that needed to be redeemed was displayed.

The logs that held up the roof and formed the ceiling were hung with buckets and shovels and lamps and saddles for sale.

At the beginning of our trading career, there had been a glass case filled with decrepit fur hats, and the rafters were hung with a few saws and shovels and buckets, all left behind by the previous owners. The back rooms were alive with weevils of some sort. So we consulted an exterminator, who sent out a supply of insecticide with instructions

Joe Toddy and Billy Tsosie

to set pans of it around on the floor. Joe Toddy, general help around the place, figured that a few pans full would work well over a weekend, but that a liberal dispersion, wetted down, would have quicker results. He dampened all the floors and closed the doors. The results were dramatic. The fumes accumulated and a spark from the gas refrigerator blew the roof sky high. When it settled crookedly down on top of the walls again, shovels, brooms, and ax handles were caught between the walls and roof. They didn't have time to sail into the unknown as the fur hats had done. We never saw hide nor hair of the hats again.

To calm the evil influences of such a catastrophe we hired old Lukaichukai to perform a rite of exorcism. All the customers who were hesitant before the ceremony were happy to return to trade again.

The area in front of the counters was known in all trading posts as the Bull Pen and was one step down from the floor in back of the counters. I suppose there was a psychological advantage in always being a few inches taller than the customers. In the Bull Pen was a wooden bench and a large wood stove. In the winter there was always a huge pot of coffee on the stove and paper cups were available for anyone who wanted. But he had to throw the used cup into the trash and not on the floor. Neither was anyone allowed to spit on the floor. We had one other strict rule: the ten-cent cans of sardines could not be opened inside the building. We simply could not stand the smell.

Several storerooms backed into the hill, and we let loose a couple of bull snakes in that area to control mice. But we did not tell our customers about these guardians. The Navajos have a reverence for snakes, and we did not know whether they would approve of the restriction of the reptiles. There were a lot of rattlers in the vicinity as there was a den not far down the arroyo where both bull snakes and

Left to right: Bill Lippincott, Philip Shorty and his wife and their child, Sallie

rattlers hibernated. We were given definite indications that we were not to harm them. I had a plan to send word to the Snake Clan of the Hopis to come get their Little Brothers for use in the Snake Dance but somehow I never got around to it. When one of our horses, a big dark raw-boned animal named Thundering Shux, was bitten by a rattlesnake right in the soft part of his nose, the nose swelled up like an oversize pudding. Shux looked just like a moose minus its antlers. Up on the hill, outside the ruins, we built a horse corral and a stone stable where snakes liked to lurk in the cool under the water trough. One year the medicine men gave us permission to eliminate the rattlesnakes, but only on one day. In two hours we killed seventeen.

Across the road from all our buildings were the government corrals and dipping vats for the annual dipping of the flocks of sheep. The corral fences were made of uneven upright tree limbs. In the east these are called picket fences, in the west coyote fences. The government branding of horses and cattle here was also an annual event.

In the wide, dry, sandy arroyo between the store and the corrals was a healthy stand of purple beeweed which was fed by seepage from our spring. Because of the beeweed and because of the flowers that I grew in the patio, there was a large population of hummingbirds. They dive-bombed us early in the summer mornings when we slept outdoors, levelling off with a whir just above our noses. Crip Chee used to hide in the tall weeds and snatch hummers with his one hand. He never harmed the little birds, and I suspect that he was gathering pollen from their backs. That pollen is a very important medicine in many ceremonies.

The kitchen and the living room both opened onto a screened porch which, in turn, opened onto a small grassy yard bordered by flower beds. Under a fragrant tamarisk tree was a stone birdbath. For two days, one summer, a Great Blue Heron stood proudly soaking his feet in the only standing bit of water he could find for miles around.

The scattered buildings of our trading post under the cottonwood trees must have been an aerial navigation landmark. The transcontinental planes always made a turn above us as they headed east or west. Maybe UFOs had us on their maps too. One noon hour in 1943, when the store was closed for lunch, a group of excited Navajos burst through the patio gate and pulled me out where I could have an unobstructed view of the sky away from the trees. Suddenly a cigar-shaped object of no particular color zoomed along—whoosh— just above the eastern horizon and disappeared to the south. The Navajo men, with upturned faces, pointed with their lips into the northern sky. There, at what seemed to be a great height, were four dark objects too far away to discern their shapes. They were moving about one another on rapid free-form paths, the way gnats do on a summer day. One shot straight up past the others and disappeared while the other three continued their erratic dance and were finally cut off by the northern horizon. What were they?

A few weeks later I was at a party in Berkeley at the home of the book editor of the San Francisco Chronicle. The literary conversation was overwhelming. Only one other guest and I were neither reporters nor book authors. He turned to the crowd and said "Did you know that Sallie saw UFOs in Arizona last month?" This was not long after a report had come out of Mexico that a UFO had landed there and little green men three feet high had climbed out of it. One of the reporters turned to me and asked, "Were there little green men three feet high in them?" "No," I said with conviction. "They were four feet high." The next day on the front page of the Chronicle was an article about four-foot-high passengers in UFOs being seen in Arizona.

As a matter of fact in 1936, long before the flap over UFOs, Bill and I had been lying in a field just south of Orinda in the San Francisco Bay area. We were watching the hawks ride the air currents above the ridge of the hill. Over us, at a height of about eighty feet, quietly floated an object that looked exactly like a huge ten-foot transparent jellyfish. It had definite globular form from which hung many strands of irregular soft material. It was transparent but had shape. It moved like a jellyfish, too, slowly undulating in a definite direction. We sat up and watched it as it floated above the dirt road where our roadster was parked. Up the valley it went while we drove along beneath it in the topless car until we came to the end of the road and could go no farther. It left us wondering what in the world it could be, and we are still wondering.

THREE

Bad Roads and Worse

The roads are paved now, and in a matter of hours you can crisscross the entire reservation. But when we lived at Wide Ruins the roads were often impassable due to mud in the fall, snow in the winter, and drifted sand in the spring. The only paved road that I remember was the floor of the bridge across the Chinle Wash en route to Kayenta. Mile after mile of tooth-jarring ruts led up to the bridge floor. Then a blissful smooth ninety yards of paving debauched us onto the muddy rutted highway again.

In early summer the roads were usually dry and passable but in July and August we had to drive with an eye out for storms. Storms not only poured sheets of water on the ground around us but also broke on the horizon at the heads of streams and arroyos. Arroyos, level areas of clean sand or smooth rock, are tempting places to camp. Many an unsuspecting newcomer to the West has lost all his equip-

Road during storm

ment and has been lucky not to lose his life by camping in an arroyo during the rainy season. Even an old hand too wise to camp in a dry wash can be fooled into trying to cross a dangerously running torrent.

During the storm season in late summer the arroyos can fill suddenly and unexpectedly. They are fed by cloudbursts in the mountains where the streams begin. When our road would disappear under madly swirling water Bill would send me wading ahead to test the depth of the water and to make sure that there was no quicksand. If all seemed safe he would gun the motor, ease the front wheels into the maelstrom, and slosh across. But one night the ordinarily dry watercourses came up quickly, one in front of us and one in back, and we were trapped on the island between. Luckily we had two

Mud

Sand

Navajo friends with us, and they set to work to peel bark from trees until they found dry wood underneath for a fire. So we cooked a scanty meal, threw our ground cloths down on the sopping ground, crawled into our bedrolls, and slept damply until morning, through we were wakened frequently by the crash and grinding of huge rocks being carried down from the mountains by the force of the water. But in twelve hours the storm had passed and only puddles were left in the wet sand of the arroyo bottoms. So on our way we finally went.

Our Ford cars and trucks were in constant need of repair. It was not unusual for the bushing in the steering wheel to be in bad condition, the frame to be broken, the wiring to have several shorts, and to have the brakes so full of sand that they were unworkable. In the back of the cars we always carried shovels, axes, chains, bedrolls, water, and a little food, and sometimes firewood if we were headed for a part of the country without many trees. Even if there were trees they were often too wet to use for fires.

En route to Chambers to pick up the mail one rainy day I drove through a large puddle that stretched from one side of the road to the other. When I came back an hour or so later the puddle was still there. Since it had been only a few inches deep and had caused no problem on the sandy road, I didn't even slow down but hit the water at full speed. Unfortunately, while I was down at the post office there had been a cloudburst in the hills to the east. The rushing water had torn through that puddle and had then subsided leaving an innocent-looking surface camouflaging a two-foot-deep ditch. The pickup came to a crashing stop, the fan cut a large round hole in the radiator, and I had to hitch a ride home in a Navajo wagon.

Once when Bill wanted to do some winter photography we decided to camp in Monument Valley. With a couple of Navajo men and a house guest who was also interested in photography, we headed west. We had deliberately chosen the week between Christmas and

New Year for the trip. It did make some sort of half-witted sense. The winter had been one of freezing and thawing, freezing and thawing, with the result that the roads were hub deep in thick, clinging mud. During this time, the heavy trucks from the wholesale houses were delivering hardware, food, clothing, and everything else that the Navajos would trade for. They had so churned up those roads that they quickly became almost impassable and could be negotiated only with chains, much shoveling, and rebuilding of a roadbed with rocks and tree branches. But during the holidays the trucks stayed in their garages and the roads were unchurned.

There was a more direct way back to Wide Ruins than the way we had come out. So, late in the evening, we turned off and headed straight southeast. If possible, side roads can be even worse than the main highways on the reservation. But the full moon rose and the radio was playing Christmas carols and we didn't think twice. Out of nowhere, across the road loomed a ten-foot high sand dune, shining a beautiful ghostly white in the moonlight. Bill backed the car a few feet, raced the engine, threw in the clutch, stepped hard on the accelerator, and buried the car in the dune. "Well, we're stuck," I remarked unnecessarily. "We're not stuck," growled Bill angrily, "we're just detained." So out we piled, those with shovels shoveling industriously, those without scraping away with cold hands. One of the Navajos remarked sotto voce, "Scorpions live in sand dunes." He didn't want to spoil the beauty of the frozen scene by saying it out loud.

To bolster our morale we built a small fire and set a pot of coffee to boil. A coyote joined us and sat out of sight on the edge of the firelight howling belligerently at us until I howled back. There was a sudden, almost physical silence and then came a tentative, questioning "Yip??" and he left us to our digging.

When possible, important ceremonies are held during the winter when evil spirits are frozen underground and are thus incapable of causing trouble. The first spring mist signals the spirits' release, when they rise a few feet above the cold weeds and grasses. So attending the intriguing Yei Bi Cheis or Night Chants with their weird but compelling falsetto songs, or the Fire Dances or Mountain Chants with their many revuelike segments, is always a cold, uncomfortable ordeal. At the Night Chant you stand around in the cold all night long watching the line of masked dancers. At the Mountain Chant, again all night, you sit on the frozen ground in the all-encompassing Dark Circle of Branches watching the dances, the magic acts, the ever-changing tempos, costumes, and moods. The dancers have an un-self-conscious grace and a sincerity of purpose that is enthralling. The Feather Dance, combining beauty and magic, was always the segment that I liked best. One of our customers once presented me with a painting that he had done of the lovely girl, hair flowing loose, stepping lightly in front of a basket in which an eagle feather stood upright and swayed in time.

The chants are not located for the convenience of the audience, and getting to one is often a matter of driving helter-skelter across country. We would post a Navajo on the hood of the pickup as pilot and he would keep a sharp eye out for tree stumps, rocks, unexpected gullies, and badger holes while the driver dodged trees and boulders. An arm flung out to the right and a sudden yelp and the steering wheel would be quickly turned to the left. An admonitory call of "Tse!" would alert us to a rock ahead and we would dodge past it without losing speed. Sometimes the car would leap onto a hump of frozen mud and we would find ourselves hung up with all four wheels spinning ineffectually until, with ax and shovel, we crawled underneath and hacked our way free. In the distance we could see, reflected in the sky, the flickering colors of the big fire around which the costumed men and women were dancing.

Before we bought Wide Ruins, while we were living in a tent at Canyon de Chelly, two photographer friends of ours from Berkeley turned up on assignment from Standard Oil. They were to photo-graph the canyon and submit pictures for a series of American scenes that the company was giving away to customers. Their little car was loaded with equipment. Up the floor of the canyon they drove, all the way to Spider Rock at the fork of Canyon de Chelly and Monu-ment Canyon. They carefully took a very dramatic picture of a black storm breaking in the sky behind Spider Rock. They should have known what to expect, but they were new to that part of the country, so they took a leisurely trip back down the canyon, stopping at a ruin or two on their way. Crossing a damp spot, the car bogged down. Unbeknownst to them, the bog was quicksand. The more they spun

I am sitting at the top of the hand and toe trail. The black dots at the bottom are people and horses around the sunken car. Photo by Cliff Bond

their wheels, the deeper they sank. Remembering that they had just passed a Navajo hogan, Cliff headed there for help while Humpy began to unload the car to lighten it. As Cliff neared the hogan a Navajo woman rushed out shouting to him. But she was speaking her own language. "The water's coming down the canyon!" Cliff thought she was telling him to get out of her cornfield so he was bowing and apologizing to her when he heard the roar of water. Humpy had heard the same sound while hoisting their big camera up onto a rock. Both men got back to the car just as a four-foot wall of water hit it. They grabbed what few things they could and climbed up to the roof. But the car sank faster and the water reached higher and higher until they were washed off into the flood. The sand-filled water soon made it impossible to swim or float so they took off their silt-laden clothes, all except their underpants. That morning on their way up the canyon, a Navajo had pointed out to them an ancient hand-and-toe trail that scaled the perpendicular cliff, and luckily they came ashore not far from its base. We found them on the rim that night, cold, shivering, and scared.

The next morning back down the hand-and-toe trail we all went. Those trails, used for centuries, are simply notches cut into the rock, just deep enough to provide holds for toes and fingers. The Indians scamper up and down them like lizards. They have even been known to dance down them. We weren't quite as carefree as the people who use them every day, but we did manage to carry shovels and canvas sacks.

All we could see of the car was the corner of the windshield sticking up above the sand. Navajos gathered around and we all set to work to dig out cameras, lenses, typewriters, notebooks, tools, and whatever else we could find. Of course everything was filled with sand and all the mechanical gadgets were permanently ruined. So was the car. It was abandoned to sink out of sight into the canyon floor.

Down the trail. Photo by Cliff Bond

Two or three years after the loss of the car, some friends from California, to whom Cliff and Humpy had told their story, visited us. They wanted to see the quicksand scene so we took them to Chinle and down the White House Trail to the bottom of the canyon. That trail is a Park Service trail and is an easy way into the canyon. We walked through the sand to the fork of the de Chelly and Canyon del Muerto and then on a mile or so to a thin, high spur of rock jutting out from the cliff wall. A talus slope hugged the base. The hand-and-toe trail that we were looking for began at the top of the talus. Peg and Tom couldn't understand how such a trail was climbable so Bill and I started up to show them. But after a few yards of slanting steps, the toe holds disappeared around the edge of the spur. With no talus on that side there was a straight drop of a hundred feet. I worked my way around to the sheer side and was catching my breath when I heard Peg say, "Oh, that's easy," and I knew what she would do. So I waited, and sure enough, around the corner came Peg. She saw the drop below her, the wind hit her and she screamed. I reached out and

Humpy and the car. Photo by Cliff Bond

Excavating the car. Photo by Cliff Bond

grabbed the back of her jacket and hung on for dear life. Luckily, Bill had a coil of rope on his shoulder. He made a loop, dropped it to me, and I tied it firmly around Peg. In precarious situations it is always easier to go up than down, so by main strength we hauled poor Peg all the way to the top of the canyon. She collapsed in a fit of hysterics. Tom had to walk out to the mouth of the canyon all by himself.

Sometimes on summer evenings we drove down to Chambers while the sun was setting. The cross lighting made every tree and rock stand out clearly. Often we could see distant hogans that we had never noticed before. Those Navajo houses, made of the materials of the land itself, are almost impossible to spot until a deep shadow gives them away. Once in a while our noses would catch the fragrance of juniper smoke from some Navajo's cooking fire. One evening three coyotes, noses to the ground, glided across the road in front of us and stopped to watch us from behind a little hill. We ourselves stopped at the top of a rise and looked out over the rolling, juniper-dotted hills to a sharp cliff in the distance, vividly washed with red by the setting sun. There was such a feeling of strong, quiet peace over all the land.

Once while driving home we were greeted by the sight of Mrs. Beaver, Big Shorty's wife, all one hundred and sixty pounds of her, sitting disconsolately beside a large pile of belongings, including her saddle. When we stopped to pick her up she yelped with delight. She had gone to Chambers to gather up some things that she had loaned to some friends. While she was there gossiping and going into detail about her current aches and pains, her horse had jerked loose from its carelessly tied rope and had hotfooted it home solo. Mrs. Beaver piled her belongings into the hatch back. She climbed into the back seat to sit beside Pretty Boy, whom we had picked up at the Chambers post office. It was Sunday evening so we turned on the car radio and the four of us were regaled with Pagliacci as we slithered through mudholes and dodged chuckholes all the way back to Wide Ruins.

When it rained the country smelled of sage and creosote and the air was cleansed of dust. I liked to wander around the hills then as long as the rain did not turn to hail. The colors in the sand and rocks were enhanced by the scrubbing that they got. I filled my pockets with bright colored pebbles that dulled again when they dried.

The edge of a storm that was attacking the eastern horizon was pelting Wide Ruins when I donned a jacket and headed for the hills in back of the post. It was late in the evening and soon became dark. In the northern distance I watched the headlights of a car coming cautiously along the ridge-top road between Klagetoh and Wide Ruins. The arroyo below us was raging with sand and rock-filled water, and I was surprised and concerned to see the headlights disappear over the edge of the arroyo and not reappear. I ran back to the house and alerted Bill, who quickly started the pickup. Off we raced to the rescue. There in the maelstrom was a station wagon, afloat but help-lessly moving down stream. Off with our boots and jackets and into the water we leapt. Two men clambered out of the car and the four of us, by main strength, maneuvered the station wagon over against the bank where the force of the current held it immobile. We pulled them out and we all laid exhausted on the bank. I sat up, looked at my companions in disbelief and said, "Dr. Kluckhohn, I presume." Sure enough, one of them was the eminent anthropologist, whom I had known in Santa Fe many years before and hadn't seen since. The two anthropologists spent the night with us and, with the help of the Navajos, dug out their stranded car the following afternoon.

During the night a bat got into their room, flying from curtain to mantel to headboard. Dr. K., in one fell swoop, grabbed my jacket, which I had forgetfully left on a chair, and threw it in the direction of the bat. But my rock-filled pockets added momentum and out the window it sailed, taking the glass and the bat with it.

Even Highway 66, the paved route from Chambers to Gallup, was fraught with danger. The paving could be washed away by one of those sudden freshets, a bridge could disappear in a flood or, most commonly, a horse, a cow, or a wagon could erupt from six-foot-high growths of sunflowers that bordered the right-of-way. In the winter the ice was treacherous. One dark night, stopping by the post on his way to Klagetoh, a friend reported that he had struck a horse as he drove along the highway. It must have been a nudging and glancing blow as he searched for the horse for fifteen minutes, striking matches and vainly poking around in the sunflowers before giving up.

An old maid cousin who had devoted her life to chaperoning groups of young ladies to Europe once came to visit us. Before she left, her way of life had changed. We had her sitting on the crossbar over a rodeo chute, timing bucking horses as they snorted their way out the gate. In the meantime, before she became acclimated, she would persistently keep an eye out for a tearoom as we drove around the reservation. She pored over a map vaguely explaining roads of the Indian Country. She was always disappointed but always hopeful, in-sisting that I was taking the wrong turn. Showing her the sights, I took her to the Petrified Forest and then on to the little town of St. Johns. Her map showed a shortcut from St. Johns to Highway 66, one I had never taken. In a gathering storm we turned north. The storm growled and flashed and was soon dumping tubs of water on us, as the road turned to slippery, greasy clay. At times the water cas-caded across in sheets so that the road disappeared completely and could be traced only by the fence posts along the way. We slipped and slithered but I didn't dare stop as there were no signs of human-ity at all for the whole sixty miles except for those fence posts. No houses, no barns, no hogans—nothing. And every time the car skid-ded sideways Cousin Mabel would grab my leg just above the knee and squeeze with the death grip of the terrified.

It didn't help that that was my driving leg (this was before the days of automatic shift). By the time we got to the highway we were both teeth-chatteringly hysterical and I could not face the prospect of more dirt road home. I phoned Bill from a filling station and begged that he come and drive us on. My right leg was black and blue for weeks.

I have a sneaking suspicion that I had something to do with Henry Ford's death. My father used to spend part of the winters at a resort near Phoenix and I would drive down to be with him for a week or two. I took the shortcut from the Navajo Reservation on that same unpaved road through St. John's and on to Show Low and Globe, crossing the Salt River and its canyon en route. One winter, I started off with a twenty-dollar bill, a tank full of gas, and a suitcase full of summer clothes. On the way, my Mercury car gave up the ghost. Luckily I was on the brink of the Salt River Gorge so I coasted down to the bottom where there was a tiny cafe, a make-shift motel with four rooms and two baths, and a garage complete with wrecking truck. I climbed out of the car, went into the cafe, ordered a cheese sandwich, and reserved a room. The garage took over my Mercury but, not having much stock-in-trade, had to send to Phoenix for replacement parts. There were no phone connections within any reasonable distance so the message for parts was sent by the one bus that went through. I was marooned in that canyon bottom for three days before my car was ready to run again. When I went to pay my bill I asked if I could pay by check, having only a twenty-dollar bill in cash. "Honey," said the motel owner, "You shouldn't be driving all over Arizona with only twenty dollars," and proceeded to give me twenty more with a sustaining cup of strong coffee.

Needless to say, my father was pretty worried about my disappearance in the middle of Apache country and confided his worry to some of the other guests at the resort. Word soon spread, and the worry was contagious. When I finally turned up there was almost a fiesta of welcome. Several guests were friends of Henry Ford and letters flew eastward mentioning the fact that it was one of his cars that had failed me. He died the following week.

Some of our more hair-raising trips were over the dirt road to the north. That was the route to the missionary hospital at Ganado and many were the Navajos whom we rushed there, badly injured, deathly sick or about to give birth. Annie Wauneka was one of the latter. Her husband, George, had come running into the store bug-eyed and pale. His wife had gone into labor but had trouble so he loaded her into a truck and, with a sublime faith in our abilities, brought her to us. But the baby arrived en route to the post and there they were out in front of the store, baby and all. However, Annie had retained the placenta and was in agony. The sand and dust were blowing. I took the baby inside and frantically phoned the Ganado Hospital for advice. I was told to put her in the back of our station wagon and get her to the hospital *quick*!! So while Bill put a mattress on the floor of the car and eased Annie onto it, I rushed around collecting sheets, blankets, and clean clothes. I wrapped the baby up in such a bundle that from then on I had trouble remembering which end was which. We managed to get to the hospital all right—the doctor said just in time— but the new mother was delirious and once I thought that she was dying. George stayed to give his wife transfusions but late that night

Sallie Lippincott holding Sallie Wauneka

he turned up at Wide Ruins half-starved and needing to be fed. The baby was named for me.

En route to his hogan one late afternoon Chester Kee's wagon hit a rock and Chester was catapulted onto the ground, hitting his head on the wagon wheel and neatly scalping himself. Crip Chee bound his head in a dirty rag, thoughtfully replacing the scalp on top of Chester's head, and brought him into the trading post. Chester's sister, Patsy, was in the store and promptly went into a fit of hysterics. We loaded Chester into the front seat of the car while Patsy and I sat in back. Bill broke the speed records heading north and we got to the hospital in the evening. Duncan Spinning was the doctor on duty, and Chester was laid out on the operating table while Dunc washed up. Patsy was relegated to the hall downstairs, but Bill and I were drafted to help with the operation. Chester was delirious. Both Bill and I had to sit on him to keep him still. The Gallup Ceremonial had taken place the week before and, as always, everyone interested in Indians had gathered in Gallup to renew friendships and to make new ones. That is the time when everyone caught up on whatever had happened during the past year. With Bill and me perched on top of Chester while Dunc Spinning neatly stitched his scalp back on we exchanged all the gossip that the three of us had collected the week before. It was a regular sewing circle. Chester recovered physically and psychologically.

Of course we made use of the Ganado Hospital ourselves once in awhile, sometimes to have porcupine quills removed from one or another of our dogs but more often for some ailment of our own. Once, with a sprained vertebra from tumbling down a cliff, I drew a large audience of Indians who watched fascinated as Dr. Spinning strapped my aching back. Bill once had an attack of hiccups that resisted anything we could think of as cure. He tried drinking water from the far side of a glass, breathing into a paper bag, hopping around on one foot, and so forth. Up to the hospital we went and again it was Dr. Spinning waiting for us. Bill was strapped to a table, Dunc climbed up, stood over him, seized his gauze-wrapped tongue in a pair of forceps and pulled with all his might. It worked and Bill, weak from hours of hiccing and from a sore tongue, was driven home again to Wide Ruins.

When the dirt road was wet with rain or melting snow the trip to the hospital was hazardous indeed. I particularly remember one time when I was driving, looking back through the rear-view mirror to see the whole road collapsing behind me. And once, luckily within fast walking distance of Ganado, I was stuck irretrievably in the mud right in the middle of the road. I had my Scotty dog, Thistle, with me, and he slept happily and maddeningly while I shoveled and spun wheels all to no avail. So I trudged down to the Ganado trading post to get help. The trader obligingly got out his pickup and drove me back to see what he could do with another shovel and two chains. But we couldn't get into my car. Thistle had wakened from his cozy snooze and, no doubt looking for me, had gone around from door to door and pushed down all the locks. Up to that moment I had loved Thistle to distraction.

FOUR

Rugs for Trade or Cash

A friend of mine persists in telling people that I taught the Navajos how to weave. That is an exaggeration. The Navajos have been weaving for hundreds of years and I am only eighty-three.

We were at Wide Ruins during the last days of the real trading posts. We were an economic boost to that area because the high prices that we were able to pay for rugs made up a great percentage of the Navajo's real income. We bought rugs for either cash or traded goods. The Navajos, ever adapters, enthusiastically fell in with our ideas of the standard of quality that their rugs should meet and today, nearly fifty years later, the rugs from Wide Ruins command high prices and are sought by museums and collectors. But it is no longer easy to ascribe a given rug to Wide Ruins as some weavers from other places on the reservation have adopted the Wide Ruins style. Even the weavers of Oaxaca, Mexico, are using Wide Ruins patterns and colors.

When my husband and I bought the trading post the Navajos in the area were making very poor rugs, the kind that were sold from knocked-together stands along Highway 66. The wool was not well cleaned or well spun. The bordered designs were the kind that had originated in Oriental rugs or were crossed arrows and swastikas, and the colors were red, black, and white—the designs and colors usually thought of as "Indian." We had seen the very beautiful rugs that the weavers at Canyon de Chelly produced, and we hoped to guide the Wide Ruins weavers into the production of beautiful rugs too. We knew they were capable of such work.

Patience was needed when dickering for a rug. In the store the weaver would trade her work for flour, sugar, velveteen, and what not. She always finished the trade by asking for five or ten cents worth of lollipops. But the transaction did not take place immediately. With the rug neatly wrapped in a flour sack, the weaver would stand inside the door for a few minutes greeting particular friends with a touching of hands. After all, a visit to the trading post is an event—an event to be savored and strung out. Sooner or later the bundle would be silently placed on the counter and one of us would unhurriedly set it on the scale.

In the past, some storekeepers bought by weight and a rug would be bought by the pound. But that ignored the aesthetic value of the piece. At Wide Ruins we weighed the bundle only to estimate the amount of wool that had been used, which we would use as a base for our judgment of its worth. With the weaver trailing along we would take the rug into a back room of the store, spread it out, and point out the good points and the occasional bad ones. The woman would not be embarrassed by an audience.

Hosteen Glish's family made some of the best rugs and were by far the most prolific weavers. Hosteen Kee's wife, Kee Chester's wife, Mary Gaddy, and Hosteen Glish's wife were among them. They al-

Kee hogan. Photo by John Collier, Jr.

ways seemed to have rugs on their looms that would command high prices. It was a joy to see what Glish's wife brought in, but for the men behind the counter it was also a trial to deal with her. She would lay the rug, still done up in its flour-sack wrappings, on the counter and arbitrarily demand a certain price. We always tried to pay as much as we thought the market would bear and made very little profit when we sold the rugs. I know that our high prices were an important incentive for the Indians to turn out the kind of rugs that we liked. But no matter what we offered Mrs. Glish, and it was often what she demanded, she would begin to weep and ask for more. This routine unhinged the men so she always tried to deal with them instead of

Hosteen Kee's wife at oven. Hogan in background

with Jean Cousins or me. We were not so easily bamboozled. Muttering to herself, she would finally agree. Nearly always, one of the purchases she made with her rug money was a Pendleton shawl. Such blankets are made in Pendleton, Oregon, for the Indian trade. There are fringed ones for women, unfringed for men. Mrs. Glish had stacks of them in her hogan, piled up against the walls or stowed away in small trunks and foot lockers.

I knew nothing whatever of weaving when we first went to Wide Ruins and I still find double weaves and two-faced rugs incomprehensible. Some of the Navajo women thought that I should learn about the craft firsthand, so they set up a loom for me and provided me with undyed yarn and the proper wooden implements. They then watched my progress with critical eyes. I dyed some of the yarn with the yellow wood of the holly berry and some with tea and set to work. The resultant rug was not one that the post would have given much cash or credit for, but I was proud of it and the women were too. It was displayed in the next trading-post rug show and looked simply

Glish hogan. Photo by John Collier, Jr.

awful alongside the ones that were expertly made. But it was the center of attention—and criticism.

Soon the demand for Wide Ruins weavings exceeded the supply. We raised our prices accordingly, and raised the amount we gave the weavers. The prices never reached the fantastic heights that rugs are

Ralph Jones's wife

A friend and I display our attempts at weaving.

Bill and Sallie examine a Wide Ruins rug in the living room.

selling for now in the 1990s, but the Wide Ruins products did command a much higher price than the average Navajo rug.

For several months during the first year at the post we refused to buy any rugs that had designs. We demanded plain stripes. We found that these were almost impossible to sell, particularly as the wool was still not clean or well spun. So all our friends got dog blankets for Christmas that year. But once the stripes were well established to the exclusion of the arrows and swastikas, we began to insist that the yarn be improved. After that aspect of the project was mastered, we hung some of the Chinle rugs from Canyon de Chelly on the store walls. We then told the customers how much we liked them and we encouraged them to do similar patterns. We would not tolerate borders, principally because of a personal reaction of mine that makes me want to jump from bordered rug to bordered rug when I encounter them on the floor.

Rug critique. Photo by Roy Pinney

We were insistent on vegetable dye colors and suspiciously questioned any woman who seemed to have used store-bought dyes. Although we did overpay when a woman would bring in a poorly made vegetable-dyed rug, we knew that she was trying. There were many failed experiments before the weavers got the hang of it. One day a crotchety old weaver came in and slammed a bundled rug down on the counter. We opened it to find, woven into one band in angry black letters, the words Vegetable Dye Rug. That one we bought. But usually when they brought in a rug that had pictures or letters in the design we asked them to take it back and reweave it. It was not that we really objected to the occasional tapestry of that kind, but the women tended to go hog-wild with such designs while we were more interested in the production of rugs that could blend in with any type of interior decor. We felt not only that the rug market could be expanded but that resale prices could be higher. And so it was proven.

Over the years we paid more and more to the weavers, yet we were always able to sell all our stock.

We never did sell rugs through the wholesale houses in Gallup. At first, when they were such low-quality rugs, we sold them to vendors who peddled them along the highway. By 1940, as they got better and

Typical Wide Ruins rug. Photo by Bill Lippincott

better, the Wide Ruins rugs had an established reputation and buyers came to the post looking for them. We sold to individuals, museums, and interior decorating shops in both the East and the West.

The Wide Ruins Navajos, both men and women, enthusiastically experimented with every possible source of dye, even dipping wool into flooding arroyos when the waters ran red or brown from violent summer storms. But plants were the principal source of dyes. Some of the old people had memories of their ancestors' recipes. Little Woman, who had been a captive of Kit Carson after seeing her family killed in Canyon de Chelly, knew of a red color that could be obtained from the lining of the skin on the roots of the juniper tree. Nashoshie Begay told of a dye that could be either red or blue, depending on how it was boiled.

This last recipe intrigued the ethnobotanists at the University of Michigan. Volney Jones sent me a stick of some sort of acid to toss into the dye pot to cause a litmus reaction. Unfortunately the acid dissolved the wool, and the Navajos and I looked on with unbelieving dismay when the stirring stick brought up a nasty mess of pink goo.

A good blue dye is almost impossible to make from any of the plants or minerals in Northern Arizona, and imported indigo was too difficult for use in the hogans. We did get some indigo once and did the dying ourselves. We then sold the dyed wool to Ralph Jones's wife. But we did not want to make the Navajos dependent on us to that extent, so we used indigo dye only once.

However, blue is very popular, and both men and women were trying to find something that would produce that color. Ralph's wife came excitedly into the store one morning to announce that she had made a really good blue dye. When I, equally excited, asked for the recipe, she said, "You know those tall plants that grow around the water tower down at Chambers? I took the roots of those and then I went up to Ganado where I knew there were some of those bushes with twisted leaves. I gathered a lot of the leaves and boiled them with the roots. Then I threw in some old flashlight batteries."

The nearest trading post to the east was Pine Springs, known for its cast silver jewelry. At the same time that we were working to improve the weaving at Wide Ruins, the Department of the Interior was involved in an educational craft program that included weaving, and one of the areas on which it concentrated was Pine Springs. The weavers at each post were encouraged and influenced by the weavers at the other. After World War II we took over the post at Pine Springs, and by that time their weaving tradition was as well established as that at Wide Ruins. The colors at Pine Springs were apt to run to pink and pale green, and motifs in the designs were smaller and the colors paler. As I see Wide Ruins rugs now in the 1990s I see that the simple designs that I admire have become more complex as well as busier.

It is unfortunate that so much judging of rugs, in fact of all craft work, is based on the technical difficulty of creating the piece and not on its aesthetic quality. The more complicated the construction, the more chance it has to win a prize. Handsome simplicity in design is often more pleasing.

Every few months we would hold a rug exhibit. We would hang our best rugs around the garden walls and all along the outside walls of the store buildings. The Wide Ruins school children were given prizes for drawing the best rug designs. Gallons of coffee and soda pop and bushels of candy and popcorn were dispensed to the crowd that poured in at the news of free eats.

Little Navajo girls always learned to weave from their mothers, and, if the mothers were indifferent craftsmen, the child would not be well taught. So we turned to the Bureau of Indian Affairs program, and found a fine weaver at Fort Wingate who would come to the school on the hill above the trading post and give lessons in carding, spinning, and weaving to the little girls enrolled there. We provided

Rug exhibits

the wool and guaranteed to buy the children's work. We paid the teacher's salary and provided portable loom frames so the children could weave outdoors during the warm weather and indoors during most of the winter. There was an unused, dilapidated building on the school grounds that we felt could be put to good use. We talked to

Class in rug design

the men who came in to trade about the possibility of restoring it so that the girls could learn weaving in one section and the boys could learn to tan hides in the other. We agreed to provide the materials if the Navajo men would provide the labor. The men were enthusiastic and were all ready to start the project. But the building was owned by the government. When we called Window Rock and told the agency what we planned, we were given a very discouraging answer by the head of education. "Get your people together," we were told, "and take them over to Coyote Canyon where the government is building a fine new building for the people there. If the Wide Ruins group doesn't do anything perhaps the BIA will sometime put a really fine building there." I said that I thought that a bad idea, that the Wide Ruins Navajos were cooperating on a program that would surely give them a usable building, and to sidetrack that would be poor psychology. Window Rock grudgingly agreed.

We asked that someone from the agency come over to see what we had in mind, but no one came. The flat roof on the building leaked badly, so the first thing we did was jack up one side to provide a gentle slope for drainage. The word of mouth "moccasin telegraph" went into action, and I soon had a call from Window Rock. "It is against the law to alter the silhouette of a government building without permission from Washington!" "Fine," said I, "I'm having dinner with the commissioner this evening in Gallup. I'll get that permission." Within two hours there was an agency representative on the premises bowing and scraping and deciding that what we were doing was admirable. So the school weaving project got under way. It is those little girls and their daughters who are the fine weavers at Wide Ruins today.

FIVE

Visitors Expected and Unexpected

Bill and I often heard, "The next time we drive to California (Phoenix, Albuquerque, Denver) we'll stop to see you." The polite response is "That would be very nice" or "Please do." I finally learned to smile vaguely and change the subject. At the drop of a hat, casual acquaintances in other parts of the country were apt to invite themselves to visit us. Nine times out of ten they actually did turn up. What they really wanted was to see life on an Indian reservation, not to visit us.

As the nearest hotel or motel accommodations were seventy miles away, we somehow felt obligated to put visitors up. Often they would extend their stay by several days.

We were lucky enough to be hosts to many people famous in their fields. Martha Graham came once. Ansel Adams, Erick Hawkins, René d'Harnoncourt, Laura Gilpin, and others came many times. Anthropologists, of course, often turned up, Ted Kidder and Clyde Kluckhohn in particular.

Roads on the reservation in those days often became nightmares to the traveler. There was snow in the winter, sand in the spring, and rain in the fall, all occasionally making driving impossible and almost always making it difficult. During World War II, drivers who had routinely maneuvered heavy trucks over the Navajo reservation roads were assigned to drive the notoriously difficult Burma Road.

For a few years, willy-nilly, we found ourselves hosts to stranded drivers of hay trucks headed for the government-backed meat-packing project north of us. The hay to feed the waiting stock was from fields in southern Arizona. In spite of our entreaties to change their schedule, the powers-that-be persisted in loading the feed early in the morning. Inevitably on those winter days the trucks arrived late in the evening or in the middle of the night when the melting snow had turned the roads to boggy mud. The heavily loaded trucks would churn their way north, the drivers probably cursing every inch of the way, but would finally give up the fight within a few miles of Wide Ruins. This repeated scenario was to our advantage as we could usually buy the hay at reduced prices.

My avoidance of the polite response failed me once. Bill, as a member of the Department of the Interior's Indian Arts and Crafts Board, was sent to Alaska to see what the Eskimos were up to, and I went along. Bad weather marooned us in Nome where the potholes in the muddy streets reminded us of the Navajo roads except that there were dog sleds instead of horses and wagons. In Nome we got to be friends with a remarkable Eskimo woman, Emma Willoya. She was the organizer of the Nome Skin Sewers, who made the clothing for the second Byrd expedition to Antarctica. When we finally left Nome, Emma came to the plane to see us off and gave me an old driftwood bowl for "a birthday present." I hugged her when she said wistfully that she hoped to see the United States sometime and I broke my rule and invited her to stay with us when she came. I thought Nome too

Emma Willoya and the cow

far away for her to ever make such a journey. But she saved her pennies, and make it she did. She was the perfect house guest. Everything interested and pleased her, and she even got up early every morning and washed our car, as a ride in the roadster with the top down was the height of excitement. At breakfast one morning Emma confided to me that her lifelong dream was to touch a cow. She gingerly realized that ambition when we took her to a dairy farm near Joseph City. During our stay in Nome we had met a young Eskimo man who drew Arctic scenes in ink on pieces of tanned skin. One day on a trip to Gallup to take part in the annual exhibition of Indian arts and crafts, we couldn't believe our eyes or ears when we heard our name called. We turned to find Henry Ahapu standing on the sidewalk with his art work and a watermelon under one arm. He almost cried in relief when he saw us, someone he knew. Weeks before he had pocketed all his money and started out to see the world, paying for his trip as he went along. A ticket he bought took him as far as Gallup and his last cent had been spent on that watermelon.

We reserved Henry a space in the exhibit hall and talked the exhibit committee into adding a special category, India ink on tanned skins, to the kinds of work to be judged. Somehow or other Henry won all the prizes in that category, which added up to just enough to get him back to Nome with his watermelon, from which he refused to be parted.

My Aunt Lalla, who was also my godmother and perhaps felt that my life in the Wild West needed looking into, came for a week's stay. She arrived in her usual high style in a Rolls Royce complete with uniformed chauffeur. This gave the puzzled Navajos the impression that she was either under arrest or under police protection. In celebration we organized a hot dog and marshmallow toast in the patio in front of the house.

The fire that we lit for the picnic drew an interested audience of Indians who clustered around on the ruin mounds around the post. There they could get a good view down into our garden area, where Aunt Lalla was seated in a large comfortable chair before a bonfire. She was initiated into the art of cooking a wiener on the end of a stick but she much preferred browning a marshmallow the same way. She soon graduated to two forked sticks and was toasting four marshmallows at a time and passing them out graciously to any Indians she could entice down off the hillsides.

One evening a stray tourist arrived at the store just as we were closing. She wedged her way in and had me show her everything in the place. Then she said that it was too bad that she wasn't buying anything. I thought it was too bad too. She talked without stopping and, every now and then, would suggest that she spend the night with us. I ignored that. She then asked if it would be all right and safe if she spread her bedroll outside the store. I replied that the reservation belonged to the Navajos and I didn't think they would object if she slept on their ground. I suggested that she go off on a side road to bed down. I herded her out and shut the door firmly on the tenth suggestion that she stay with us. Next she hied herself to the Cousinses' house and went through the same process with them. She talked to Bill C. for ten minutes without getting anywhere and then said pointedly, "Some traders are very nice people." Bill agreed and then added, "Some of us aren't very nice, too." She bedded down outside the store right alongside the main road. Next morning she was gone.

Dick and Doc arrived at Wide Ruins one summer afternoon in a beat-up old car with Maryland license plates. Doc was a professor at a college in Baltimore and Dick was one of his students. They pulled up in front of the store just as we were closing for the day, so of course they had dinner with us. Their unexpected arrival was explained by the fact that a mutual friend had told them to consult with us and then had forgotten to tell us they were coming. During dinner we learned that they were planning to make a trip on horseback from Flagstaff to the Rainbow Bridge, a long trip across a desolate part of the Navajo Country. Neither of them had ever been on a horse, so they had sent for instructional government pamphlets and had been practicing riding and packing on barrels in the back yard in Baltimore. We took a dim view of their plans and pointed out the dangers of such a trip. But, experienced in Hollywood westerns, they were convinced that we, like all westerners, were kidding a couple of dudes. They had planned a Wild West experience and, by gum, they were going to have it.

We felt that if we let them go we would be responsible for a tragic accident to a couple of very nice young men. So we put a plot of our own into operation. We saddled up four horses and invited Dick and Doc to go with us to visit some hogans. Within two hundred yards of the corral both had fallen off their mounts. So they thankfully stayed at Wide Ruins all the rest of the summer. They rented two horses from the Navajos and learned a lot about horses that the government pamphlets hadn't mentioned. Never tie a horse to an empty bucket, for example.

A trading post, or any building of any consequence at all out on the reservation, is a matter for curiosity. Although we were not on a tourist-traveled road, once in a while a car would stop and people would wander in, look us over critically, and walk out again. Occasionally they even opened the gate to the patio and came into our private area. That always made us mad, but I suppose we were touchy. One summer Sunday I was puttering around the patio and a house guest was writing letters in the living room. In the back part of the house was a door that opened from the vegetable garden to the bedrooms. It was difficult to get to, as you had to go out from the house in the first place or else climb a wall to get to the garden. Nevertheless that Sunday afternoon a perfectly strange non-Navajo man came wandering in through that back door. He went through the bedroom, down the hall, through the library, and out through the living room to the front door, tipping his hat to the astounded letter writer as he passed. He didn't even nod to me as he made his way to the gate, climbed into a car, and drove away.

A small number of trading posts, such as Goulding's in Monument Valley and the Thunderbird Lodge at the mouth of Canyon de Chelly, had motel accommodations for guests. Therefore, it was not too surprising when a woman came up to our exhibit booth during the weekend of the Gallup Ceremonial, introduced herself and a friend, and announced, "When the Ceremonial is over we are coming out to Wide Ruins for a few days." I smiled politely, and said, "I'm sorry but we don't have accommodations for guests." It jarred me to have her state, "Oh, we know that. But you must have a guest room." Somewhat testily I replied, "No, we don't." Somewhat testily herself she said, "We can sleep on a couch in the living room." "We don't have

Photo by L. Leba

a living room," I lied. "Well then,"—angrily—"We'll bring bed-rolls and sleep in the stock room." At that my own anger took over. "We don't have a stock room," I growled. She turned, red-faced, and snarled, "Well, we'll spread our bedrolls in the yard. At least you can be that hospitable." I'm glad to say they never showed up.

The old Indian who lived in Canyon del Muerto at the foot of a cliff decorated with pictographs of Spanish-introduced animals (including a large painting of a cow) was an ultraconservative dresser. Thus he wore the once-stylish trousers made of cotton calico. His home address was Standing Cow and the name he went by was Calico Pants. He wasn't exactly a house guest at Wide Ruins when he and his family arrived one afternoon in a beat up wagon pulled by a bedraggled team of pinto horses. Because it was Sunday the store was closed. The Pantses spread their blankets, built a fire, broke out a frying pan and a soot-blackened coffee pot, and settled down under a cottonwood tree to wait until they could do some trading on Monday. But they had traveled a long way from Standing Cow and seemed to be short on food, so we opened the store to them and in they piled.

They had brought a well-woven rug with them. I have always considered the Chinle rugs of that time the handsomest of all Navajo weavings, and we offered them a very good price. They took so much to trade out that it was dark before they finished. There was to be a lunar eclipse that night and I didn't want to miss it. I left the last of the trading to Bill and went outside to look at the sky. The eclipse had begun, and the familiar store, the cottonwood trees, the sheep corral, and the gas pumps looked ghostly and strange. The scene looked the way your own lighted room looks strange when seen through a window. An old woman, Calico Pants's daughter, followed me out and looked around round-eyed and speechless. Navajos don't point with their fingers so with my lips I pointed to the moon. She took one horrified look, screamed, and threw her arms around my neck. I muttered encouraging words, patted her on the shoulder, and led her back in to the post where she sat on the bench sobbing in fear. The whole family huddled in a corner by the stove until we judged the phenomenon must be over. We assured them that their medicine men had taken care of the situation and the crisis was past.

Not all of our guests were unexpected drop-ins. Many were actually invited. One who came to Wide Ruins several times was a man who appreciated beauty wherever it is found. We were most anxious to have him see a ceremony in which there was to be a sand painting. We felt he would admire the strange patterns formed by the traditional figures and would marvel at the intricacy with which the painting is done: the careful dribbling of colored sand between thumb and index finger of each assistant to the medicine man is used to form conventionalized gods, plants, and animals.

A sand painting forms part of many ceremonies and is constructed during the day and then is destroyed before the sun goes down. Nez Ben's mother-in-law and daughter were having a nine-day ceremony during which time there were to be five different sand paintings on

Nez Ben with wife and child

five different days. This day was to be the biggest and best, so for two weeks we planned to go that day.

At fairs and other exhibits the casual tourist may often see a Navajo or two making a simulation of a sand painting, and they are really interesting to see even there. The work is as carefully and as well done as during an actual ceremony. But the true essence of the painting is dependent upon the chanting, the meticulous supervision of the medicine man, the hogan setting and smoky air, and the occasional comment or friendly joke by one of the absorbed painters. (The Navajos do not feel that religion is a solemn thing which forbids laughter and gaiety. In fact the clown is a revered personage and may ridicule even the Yei, the god, himself. When the People were slowly working their way to this world from the dark, unpleasant underworlds it was

Sand painting. Photo by Cliff Bond

the clowns and their antics that made them laugh and bolstered their spirits. If it had not been for laughter, the People would have despaired and would never have reached their present level of attainment.)

As I had seen the sand painting that was to be done for Nez Ben's family before, I knew that it was elaborate and impressive and I knew that our friend would be enchanted. After the complex pattern of the painting itself is dribbled out in colored sands on the smooth base of yellow earth, wooden birds are hung above it. They are made to swing back and forth and, while they are thus flying, the men imitate their songs on shrill whistles. A wooden snake slides below the birds.

We went down to Nez Ben's hogan after lunch. We were told that we could not enter the ceremonial hogan just then so we went into the hogan where the women were cooking a meal. They were boiling mutton, and grilling goat ribs, and baking round yellow rolls.

The afternoon wore on and we were still not told to come to the

Sand painting. Photo by John Collier, Jr.

other hogan. I was not surprised that I was not to see the painting being made, as Navajo women must not be witness to such a thing and the Indians seemed to think that I had been among them long enough so that allowances no longer need be made for me. I was expected to behave as they behaved. I was glad that I had already gotten in my sightseeing before their mores clamped down on me.

But we could not understand why the men were not called in. We sat around the hogan on benches and on the floor. I was given a place of honor on the bed beside Nez Ben's pretty daughter. She and her grandmother were bedecked in all their finest clothes and jewelry as the sing was being performed for them. All ceremonies are curing ceremonies in one way or another, as the Navajo believe that illness is caused by being out of accord with the Way of Life. To maintain or regain rapport, one must have a ceremony. I don't know the detailed reason why the old woman and her granddaughter felt that a sing was needed but undoubtedly it was because they had been sick in the past or expected to be sick in the future. If they neglected this ceremony, their descendants one or two generations hence could bear the brunt of the anger of the gods for such negligence, ill could befall an innocent person because of the neglect of his ancestors. It was obvious that the two women were not being harried by any disease or worry at the moment. They were both in blooming health and were proud and pleased as punch to be the center of so much important activity.

After some idle chatter, somehow or other we became involved in making cat's cradle patterns out of old pieces of string. The women were enchanted that I knew some of the same patterns they knew. I had learned them when I was at the University of Chicago from a man who had learned them in turn from some Australian natives among whom he had been doing ethnological work. Many of the most intricate and complex figures that can be made with a looped piece of string, woven in and out and twisted back and forth by the fingers, are known and played with by peoples all over the world. The evidence of this never ceases to astonish me. That the knowledge of how to build and light a fire, how to plant and cultivate crops, how to chip flint and grind stone into useful implements, and other basic items of learning should be universal I can well understand.

But how can it be that innumerable seemingly meaningless designs made only for entertainment with a piece of string or a strip of rawhide can be known step by step by all native people everywhere? Such an important invention as the wheel was not known by everyone a few hundred years ago. But cat's cradles were. Native people on this side of the Pacific, and only on this side of the Pacific, planted and harvested corn that had taken them from the dawn of civilization to develop.

Over in Asia other native people planted and harvested wheat and oats and other foods that were never known to pre-Columbian Indians. Yet both of them, after the hoeing and weeding were done, would sit down in the evenings and idly make exactly the same string figures by twisting their fingers through dozens of steps to reach the final design. They even go through identical steps in untangling the patterns.

The string figures went on, with the Navajos teaching me some I didn't know. A notable one that Gee Bah patiently taught me is the most difficult one I have tried. It takes careful manipulation and numberless changings of string from finger to finger before the final result is achieved. That result is an anticlimax. After all the hullabaloo and bated breath while the figure is being composed, all that comes out of it are two lines of string up and down between two other lines of string back and forth. The name of that figure is Standing, a forthright and simple name for a forthright and simple design. We did other named figures: Coyotes Running Away From Each Other, Many Stars, a Hogan, a Bird's Nest, the Morning Star, the Horned Star, a Loom Frame, and some whose names I forget.

Bill had wandered outside for some fresh air while all this was going on. When he came back he looked rather thunderous but I was too bent on learning Standing to really take in the expression on his face. Pretty soon he said quietly to me across the fire, "I have just had word from Kinlichine, the medicine man." I asked vaguely, "What did he say?" "The word is Pay or Stay Away," said Bill angrily. I was horrified. For it to have happened to a tourist who would just be passing through the country would have been bad enough but for such a demand to be made to us was more than we could stand. I threw down my piece of string, said loudly and I hope impressively, "That is a bad thing," and Bill and I stalked out the door.

We came home hell bent for leather and our horses must have thought we were crazy. We were hurt and angry and embarrassed that the occasion had fallen so flat. Our only consolation was that the medicine man was not a local citizen but had been imported for the performance. However, he was often called in on cases at Wide Ruins and he at least knew who we were. Our guest, whom we had particularly wanted to see the ceremony, was disappointed but he felt that we had all done the right thing in decamping in high dudgeon.

When Bill Cousins heard what had happened he got even madder than we were. He promptly went out into the middle of the trading post and bawled out all the Navajos who were there. That they were completely innocent and hadn't been within five miles of the offending medicine man had nothing to do with it. He bawled them out anyway. He hoped that part of Kinlichine's fees were paid to him in naltsos, the paper credit slips we gave to a customer who had not traded out the full amount due for a rug or a sheep or whatever he had brought in to trade. Bill Cousins said he would refuse to cash the medicine man's naltsos and what is more he would charge him double for anything he bought for cash. He also worked up a pretty scathing speech to deliver at an appropriate moment, when there were a lot of customers in the store.

I think that the local Navajos were pretty much embarrassed by the occurrence. Patsy Martin told me that the women in the cook hogan said that we should have gone in anyway and not paid any attention to Kinlichine. The next morning Hosteen Yazzi, who fancied himself somewhat of a local chieftain (and I guess he is so far as anyone can be a chieftain among the individualistic Navajo), came in and made a speech to us about how all the men in the ceremonial hogan, when they heard of Kinlichine's demand, told him that it was not right and that we were to come in anyway. "But," said Hosteen Yazzi, "You move too fast. You already gone."

SIX

Between Gallup and Chambers

Gallup, New Mexico, a rough town with no pretensions of being anything else, was seventy miles away from Wide Ruins. We did our banking there, and the wholesale companies (primarily Gross Kelly) were the source of stock for the store: canned food, clothing, hardware, candy, saddles, wagons, and other items. Every few weeks representatives of the wholesale companies toured the reservation, stopping at each post to take orders for goods to be delivered by truck.

Like any housewife, I kept a list of things to be shopped for next time I went to town, things not supplied by Gross Kelly. But we made those trips only once a month or less and by that time it often seemed that many of the things on the list were no longer needed. Of course having a general store just on the other side of the kitchen door made that list a short one to begin with.

A trip to town was a special event. While Bill conducted business I haunted the railroad station, meeting the passenger trains that paused there in their hurtling journeys east or west. It was fun to watch the passengers stroll the platform. The moo of a diesel engine or the hysterical howl of a steam locomotive anxious to be on its way called them back to the cars and whisked them off east or west. It was even more interesting to watch the colorful people who bustled, sauntered, strode or staggered on the streets of Gallup. There were tourists, of course, staring with interest or apprehension at the Indians from Zuni Pueblo or the far-flung Navajo reservation; ranch hands in high-heeled boots and dusty Levis; housewives and businessmen; railroad gangs and, once in a while, a Hollywood movie crew out on location.

I was always entranced by the variety of individuals making up the crowds on the sidewalks. There were Navajo women in full sweeping skirts and velveteen blouses, one carrying two large packages and licking an ice-cream cone; a shawled and moccasined Zuni woman entering the doors of the bank; a Navajo parachute jumper in uniform, proud and alone; a Navajo sailor, one of a group of silently striding Indians.

In the drugstore Bill was approached by a Navajo. "You are my friend," the Indian stated flatly although Bill had never seen him before. "You are going to lend me twenty dollars to go to Albuquerque." When Bill refused to fall in with this plan, the Navajo dug into his pocket, pulled out a crumpled leather medicine pouch, and offered it as a pledge for the loan. But before Bill could respond to that deal the Indian had a sudden shift of feelings. Angrily eyeing Bill, he blurted out, "No, this is mine. My girl friend made it for me and you can't have it. I'll walk to Albuquerque before I sell this. That's what I'll do. I'll walk." With a horrendous frown, out the door he went, headed east.

The local radio station occasionally livened up its programs by taking a microphone out onto the streets and drafting passers-by to answer questions or to give their views of ongoing events. I dodged an outthrust mike and the woman in back of me was trapped instead. "Now I am going to ask you a riddle," the interviewer said. "The answer is the name of a famous natural feature in North America. Are you ready?" The woman bridled and simpered and nodded her head. "I am big. Make no mistake. I am a superior freshwater lake. Who am I?" A thoughtful pause, and a wrinkled brow. Then her face cleared, "Yellowstone Park!" she announced triumphantly.

At Wide Ruins we could get two stations on our radio, one from Gallup and one from Albuquerque. From Albuquerque we once got news of a breakout at the state prison in Santa Fe. One of the escapees was a man who was serving time for killing a cow. I was rather intrigued by the news and rooted for him to dodge his pursuers. He had killed that cow with a crossbow. He eluded the posse for weeks, but two or three times a day there was a progress report. "He is an experienced mountain man. He eats his meat raw and makes his own snow shoes." I was sad when they finally caught him.

El Navajo, the Harvey Hotel next to the station, was the meeting place for individuals in town from the Navajo and Pueblo reservations and the outlying ranches. Occasionally we would spend the night there but, being accustomed to the quiet of the Navajo Country, it seemed that the trains were rerouted through our bedroom as we tried to sleep.

I was particularly charmed by an elderly couple who came to town once in a while and always ate at El Navajo. He was neatly togged out in white shirt and dark gray suit, the coat of which buttoned up almost to his chin. His ankle-high shoes had elastic sides. The woman's dress was what I think of as bombazine, a rustly shiny black material that must have been made into the tight-waisted dress at least fifty years before. The boned lace collar held her chin upright and the long skirt almost hid her high-topped shoes. With great pomp and ceremony they would be seated at a table in the dining room and napkins would be spread elegantly across their laps. When the meal was served they completely ignored their forks and spoons and devoted their efforts to eating with their knives alone.

They lived some miles east of Gallup, near the main line of the Santa Fe Railroad. Bill Cousins had once worked for them for a few years and during those years he developed an interest in playing the accordion. So he ordered one from the Sears catalogue. There was no regular mail delivery at that lonely outpost. If, by chance, anything did come by post, it was simply thrown off the mail car as the train hurtled by. Three times this proved disastrous to the accordion, so Bill finally gave up his musical ambitions.

In August the annual Indian Ceremonial took place in Gallup. Indians and traders, collectors and sight-seers poured into town from all points of the compass. In the morning the many Indian tribes, each group decked out in native dress, paraded through town. It sometimes happened that one of the passenger trains would be carefully winding its way along the tracks that paralleled the two main streets. After leaving Highway 66 Street the route of the parade crossed the tracks to the Ceremonial grounds. When the train stopped it neatly cut the parade and (often one tribal group) in two. Not to be interrupted the drummers and chanters would hunker down and continue their chant while on the other side of the stalled train the dancers would continue their steps to the rhythm. I expected to see the train list from port to starboard as the intrigued passengers rushed from one side to the other to stare out the windows.

There were times when we had to get a message to someone in Gallup. A phone call would have been easier than a round trip of 140 miles, but the phone system was erratic. We had a ring-down that ran the many miles to the hospital switchboard at Ganado, then over the Defiance Plateau to the agency at Window Rock, and then finally plugged into the Bell system at Gallup.

Our phone line tapped into the government line that connected the Wide Ruins school (a mile away on a lonely hill) with the half-dozen government houses and the trading post at Klagetoh and then to the Presbyterian mission hospital at Ganado. For a year or two there was a teacher at Wide Ruins, the woman who had stated airily that she "learned the Navajos to speak English," who occasionally cranked out the two long rings that were our signal and then, when we answered, aggressively demanded, "Who is this?" If Bill was the one to receive the blast he would reply a variant of "The King of Peru. Who are you?" If I was the one on the line I always asked, "To whom do you wish to speak?" This always seemed to have a quieting effect.

Of course it was often a comfort to know that there were a number of people always within ring-down reach. There were times when a frantic need to reach the hospital elicited no response and a helpful voice would come over the wire, "You must be tired. Let me try to reach them for you." Then the cranked-out ringing would be taken over by a helpful if distant neighbor.

Actually getting a call through that maze of amateur and careless wiring was often a matter of luck. The switchboard at Ganado was not manned at all hours, and a ring being answered depended on whether or not a busy nurse was within earshot and knew how to deal with the plugs. Sometimes the operator at Ganado and the one at Window Rock were miffed and would not speak to one another, thus completely cutting off any communication for anyone else. Then we would find ourselves in the pickup headed for Chambers, where there was a telephone on the Bell system. Sometimes it was more practical to go all the way into Gallup.

Late one afternoon there was a long distance call for Bill. When he answered he was told "Washington calling." Then the line fell down. So off to Gallup he rushed and somehow managed to trace the interrupted call to the Indian Arts Board of the Department of the Interior. At midnight he burst into our bedroom, woke me excitedly, and ordered, "Get up. We're leaving for Alaska in four hours." Leave for Alaska we did, all the way to inside the Arctic Circle with a suitcase full of hastily packed mismatching clothes. We did a quick survey of arts and crafts of the Indians and Eskimos of that territory and made many friends whom I still enjoy today.

When our business in Gallup was attended to we headed west along Highway 66, passing signs advertising "Petrified Aspern Wood and Beans for sell" and one that snarled in a deep growly voice "Don't pass no tax."

Chambers, Arizona, was then a town with a small store, a water tank, a railroad telegraph office, and a scattering of six or eight houses. It was the spot on the highway where the traveler left the paved road and turned north to Wide Ruins and Ganado. A crisp red, white, and blue flag flew over a very small wooden shack, proudly identifying a United States Post Office. About once a week, if the weather was good, we drove down to get our mail unless it had already been picked up and dropped off to us by some helpful truck driver.

The main line of the Atchison, Topeka and Santa Fe railroad went through Chambers. Jimmy Hill manned the railroad office there. He was the one who sent our telegrams, collected our mail, and flagged down the trains when we wanted to get on them. As a hobby he collected pencils and when I would sometimes go sailing through Chambers from east to west on the train I would throw off the pencils that I had gathered for him on our travels.

At special request the passenger trains would come to a puffing stop in Chambers to let someone get off or get on. I well remember the consternation of other travelers in my car when I would insist on climbing off the train in the middle of nowhere in the dark of the night. "Are you sure you want to leave us here?" "Is there someone out there to meet you?" "Isn't this Indian country?"

Charlotte, a writer of children's books, a handsome, intimidatingly dignified woman, planned to visit us at Wide Ruins on a train trip between her publisher in New York and her home in California. A very early stop in Chambers was arranged and I drove the eighteen miles to the railroad while it was still dark. As happy as I was at the prospect of seeing Charlotte, I did not look forward to the long trip home with her before she had had her usual morning cup of coffee, and I knew that at such an early hour there was not much chance that one would be provided. I knew her well enough to know that her mood would not be the best. Before the train came in I built a bonfire beside the tracks and set my camp coffee pot to boil. In came the train. The porter set his little stool at the foot of the steps and down those steps came Charlotte, dressed elegantly in her New York outfit. She glared belligerently at the stock corrals, at the leaking water tank, at the surrounding desert, and at me. With no word of greeting I held out a tin cup of just-made coffee. The porter was convulsed so Charlotte glared at him too. As she drank the coffee it was obvious that the morning was becoming brighter in every way and at the last drop she snatched off her mink stole, threw it down by the tracks, and pronounced, "Oh boy! The West! It's wonderful!"

Jimmy retired, and a tall talkative individual took his place and manned the telegraph key. To see if there were an express shipment for us, I went down one morning, wended my way sedately between the freight cars, and stepped daintily over the rails. Before I reached the screen door to the switch office I was greeted with, "Well, my God! Am I seeing things? A lady!" I smiled in the restrained way proper to a well-bred individual in such a situation and said in my most genteel voice, "Are there any packages for Wide Ruins?" "I don't know," says he, "I'm so busy I'm going crazy. Everybody wants something different. There's the telegraph to listen to and the trains to get through the switches. Then people come down here looking for packages!" He indicated a sheaf of papers. "There are the bills on a hundred boxes of things that are in that warehouse over there and I haven't even had time to see what is there yet. The trains keep coming through here so fast. The telegraph always has something to say. The mail has to be picked up. I tell you I just can't stand it. This morning I went for a walk down the tracks just to get away from it all." That stretch of track never seemed safe to me again. From that time on I felt that I should detour around Chambers by bus.

It was from the stock corrals at Chambers that we loaded our sheep into the double-deck railway stock cars that delivered them to feed lots in Colorado or Kansas. At the end of the buying season there was an important decision to be made: we could truck the animals to the railroad for shipping to feed lots or herd them across country. The weight to be gained or lost during transport was the deciding factor. Livestock riding bunched up in a truck would certainly lose weight. If it were decided to drive them slowly across country they would gain as they grazed, but it was only practical if the few springs en route were flowing. One year during a prolonged drought we had reluctantly decided to truck the sheep. We sent out a runner to instruct our herders to bring their charges into the Wide Ruins corrals. Much to our dismay the runner returned to tell us that two days before, the men driving the sheep had started for the railroad, making the decision themselves. Our dismay conveyed itself to our customers, who consoled us with the prediction that it was going to rain and fill up the springs and the depressions where water could accumulate. Looking at a deep blue cloudless sky, we expressed our doubts, but we were reassured that it would certainly rain that night. Of course it would, they said. They had seen me washing pinyon nuts, a sure way to bring rain. I had washed so many that there was certain to be a ground soaker. Sure enough, that night we woke to the sound of approaching thunder and the pelting of rain on the roof. The flock made it to Chambers in fine shape.

SEVEN

A Day at the Trading Post

There were nineteen customers in the trading post. All of them were standing around in perfect silence, while Bill and I stood in back of the counter feeling more and more that we were expected to stage a floor show. I suggested card tricks, but Bill declined, so we simply stood and stared back at the customers. Utter silence. An occasional cough or sniffle and then silence again. A young boy moved from the candy counter over to the loafers' bench. A baby looked around solemnly, discovered his brother had moved, and toddled over to stand between his brother's knees. Silence again, with a static quality in the very air. The Sleeping Beauty spell seemed hard to break. No one wanted to make the first move and there seemed no reason for anyone to do so. Finally Atsonie Tso reached forward with one moccasined toe and pushed an empty glass jug two inches across the concrete floor. Eyes shifted slowly toward the bottle then back again. Bill

Hosteen Glish. Photo by L. Leba   *Mrs. Glish. Photo by L. Leba*

yawned and, reluctant to break the trance, caught Hosteen Glish's eye and pointed to the bottle with his lips. In slow motion Hosteen picked up the bottle and went out the door to the kerosene shed.

The spell was broken. With a sigh Atsonie Tso tugged off a turquoise ring and offered it in payment for the kerosene. Suddenly a lively discussion, initiated by Bill, broke out on the advisability of Glish's wife making Hosteen a pair of pants out of the flowered pink cotton crepe that had come in on the last truck from the wholesalers.

John Joe suggested that my dog be sheared and the wool sold to the trading post. It was decided that after two such shearings Shadrach would grow a fine crop of hair, something really worthwhile. It was hinted that that was where some of the wool we had been selling to the weavers came from.

Mrs. Gold Tooth Number One shyly sidled up to me, leaned across the counter, and whispered, "Ex . . ." I couldn't think of any

Navajo word like that so assumed she was speaking English and got a dozen eggs out of the refrigerator. But that was not what she wanted. She kept repeating "Ex" until she pointed out a bundle of axes standing in a corner.

Frank Seven stood by the candy counter pulling out the few hairs on his chin with a pair of home-made tweezers. Like all Indians, Frank had scant facial hair, so this occasional tweezing was all the shaving he needed. He had come in to get his weekly paycheck from the Santa Fe Railroad. The Navajos who had worked on the railroad during the war got retirement checks. They had to fill out involved forms with each check, so they came into the trading post where we would do it for them. Then all they had to do was sign their names. Bill found Frank's papers and filled in the blanks while Frank watched him intently and critically. When all the spaces except the last were filled in, Bill turned the paper around on the counter and held his pen out to Frank. Pompously Frank reached into a pocket and brought out a spectacle case which he opened with great deliberation. He thoroughly polished his glasses, first one side and then the other before adjusting them carefully on his nose. With pursed lips and a wrinkled brow he scanned the paper line by line. Finally with a great flourish he grasped the pen rigidly in his fingers and slowly signed a wobbly "X."

Then, maddeningly, after the suspended animation of the past hour, everyone wanted to trade at once. Little Shorty's wife quietly pushed a credit slip across the counter and whispered one word, "Bah." Then, getting up courage, she added, "Toh da shoshie." Bread and pop. She was a pretty little thing but so shy that she wouldn't bring the dolls that she made into the store. Instead she wandered smiling into our bedroom before we were up in the morning, offering her box full of dolls. Her husband herded her along encouragingly.

Atsonie Tso wanted to have a can of sweet potatoes, some coffee, a sack of flour and a can of baking powder on the balance due on her ring. Nashoshie Begay had two coyote skins and one worthless badger pelt that he wanted to exchange for a sack of flour, baking powder, three jars of jam, and some canned milk. Yellowshirt thought he should be advanced some groceries on the sheep that he was going to shear in the spring. John Joe took up his favorite winter sport of constructing intricate cat's cradles from an old piece of string. During the summer John had to forego whatever joy he got from these string tricks, because it is only during the winter (when the spiders are spinning in the hogans) that it is safe to make such figures. Poor old Tson Yazzi told us in an earnest whisper that she had not had any food in her hogan for three days. So we gave her a box of assorted groceries and made a mental note to speak harshly to her bootlegging husband and son.

Mrs. Glish laid a bundle on the counter. Bill shot a brief pleading glance at me and tried pointedly to ignore her. I stepped up, untied the flour-sack wrapping, and weighed the rug on the store scales. I took the rug back into the rug room and spread it out on the floor. The corners lay flat and edges were straight, the soft pastels of the vegetable dyes were clear and clean, and the design was simple and pleasing. All in all it was a nice rug, so I met the asking price of eighty dollars. Mrs. Glish had followed me. Stunned and angry at not having demanded more, she glared at me and muttered under her breath, "Five dollars more." "Eighty dollars," I repeated sternly in a tone of finality. Mrs. Glish, decided that tears were of no avail when dealing with one of her own sex, went back into the store still muttering.

As I was tagging her rug, Bill brought in another one. The weaver was not one of our steady customers. She had made an attempt to weave the kind of rug we wanted. The dyes were vegetable and there was no border around the edge. Thunderbirds and crossed arrows alternated with zigzags and triangles in a dizzy pattern. Bill called the woman back to the privacy of the rug room, explained to her the good and bad points of the rug, and then offered her forty dollars for it. She was not pleased but did not argue. She seemed to be pondering Bill's criticisms and resolving to do better next time. In a burst of educational zeal, I showed her the whole pile of our best rugs and then took her into the house so she could see the ones we had kept for ourselves.

Every few weeks salesmen from the wholesale companies in Gallup would make the rounds of the trading post to take orders for depleted items and to show sample of new products. One of these men had come in while I was gone and had put his opened sample case on the candy counter. Old Hosteen Yazzi was helping himself to a cup of coffee from the large copper pot on the heating stove when his eye fell upon the open case. He sidled over to take a look at the new goodies and there was a large pink celluloid baby rattle. Hosteen could not resist. The temptation was too great. He snatched out the rattle, grasped it firmly and, with a piercing cry of the Yeis, started up and down the floor chanting the "Ho-o-o-Ho" of the Yeibitchei ceremony. He wouldn't let us put the rattle back until we assured him that we would order a dozen and that he could have his choice.

In the meantime, Glish's wife was trading out her eighty dollars. She had received credit ahead on the strength of this rug. Bill deducted the amount she owed. That included the cost of the raw wool, which she had bought from us when she first decided to weave her rug. With three of her remaining dollars Mrs. Glish took one of her bracelets out of pawn. She toyed with the idea of taking a necklace and another bracelet or two out. She would like to cut a swath at a curing ceremony that would start tomorrow, but the gathering there wouldn't be a large one and perhaps it would be more fun to buy a length of velveteen for a new blouse. Her two old blouses had been washed so many times that the velveteen looked more like soft, unironed denim. But, first she had to buy the necessities: a sack of flour and its accompanying can of baking powder, a sack of sugar and a package of shortening, so essential for making fried bread, twenty-five cents worth of oranges and half a bale of hay, some candy for the children, and a bottle of pop for herself. The essentials out of the way, she could then spend a joyful hour or two in buying sheer fripperies.

Perhaps she thought that buying a box of lined writing paper would be a grand gesture, indeed, and might impress the traders. Of course, neither Glish nor his wife could write a single word, but they could have their grandson who had been to school print a message for them. Then maybe the trader would address the envelope and send it off to their nephew, a private in the Marines in someplace called California. The elderly lady composed the letter in her mind: "Dear Nephew, Today, while I have nothing to do, I write a short word to you. Everything here are fine. How are you? Answer back soon."

Then she went to the grocery shelves to choose a can of peaches, two cans of tomatoes, some canned meat, and some beans. If only this were watermelon season, she could buy a nice big melon. Watermelons are one of the good things about summer.

Mrs. Glish bought things one by one. Thus the pleasures of trading could be savored: having money to spend, examining the shelves stocked with goods, choosing the things on which to spend, meeting friends and relatives in for their bit of trading, and watching the antics of the white people who are the traders. After each purchase, money was passed over the counter and the correct change was made. Often an Indian had only a naltsos, a little piece of paper saying that so much money was due. But buying with a naltsos definitely lacks the verve of trading with actual cash. Again Mrs. Glish pondered the advisability of taking out some of her pawn. Nothing of hers had been in anywhere near the thirteen months that these traders kept things before beginning to heckle the owners to take them out. Then usually a couple more months, at least, would go by before the dead pawn was actually sold. Mrs. Glish felt that it must be awfully inconvenient for white people not to have a pawn shop in connection with their general store. Where did they cache their valuables when they were not using them? It was nice to know that jewelry, saddles, ceremonial baskets, and buckskins were safely locked up in the trading post safe, and that they could be recovered at the same value at which they were put in.

Mrs. Glish shook hands limply and stoically with Red Man's Wife, who had come in half an hour earlier. Her son had been kicked by a horse, and she could not make up her mind whether to ask the trader to phone the mission hospital or to phone to a neighboring trading post, where there was a medicine man who knows the right chants and sand painting to cure injuries caused by a horse. She finally decided on the medicine man. She really had more faith in him. Also, she could probably count on the trader to use his car as an ambulance if the medicine man's prayers were not effective.

Apparently Glish's wife decided against redeeming more of her pawn. She had been eyeing a turquoise ring in the showcase. It was a new ring, made two weeks earlier at our other trading post at Pine Springs up on the mountain. It had tickled Mrs. Glish's fancy, and now she bought it with the last of her eighty dollars. A new ring would enhance her prestige at the sing more than would some of her old things.

Satisfied at last, but glaring angrily at us for not giving her the extra five dollars, Mrs. Glish packed all her purchases into an old flour sack and strode out the door and down to the corral to her horse. Next week she would be back again running up a grocery bill against the next rug, but for today, her trading was done.

EIGHT

Christmas at Wide Ruins

It hadn't seemed much like Christmas. The weather had been too warm and gray. But on the twenty-third Paul went out to gather cedar branches for decorating the house and the store, and trading post customers began to look expectant.

He appeared with an armload of mistletoe that he had laboriously gathered from the tops of juniper trees. He was particularly proud of one perfectly round ball, and that was tied with red ribbon and hung in the middle of the living room ceiling.

John Joe loaned his team and wagon and off we all went to cut a Christmas tree up in the canyon. The canyon bottom was rough and full of rocks, and the return trip at a brisk trot gave me second thoughts about my lifelong ambition to ride in a kangaroo. But the big pinyon tree survived the jolting and we set it up with guy-wires on the hill above the trading post. Several hundred feet of electric

Poster

wire from the diesel generator supplied power to a dozen strings of lights. Bill Cousins was drafted to put the white light on the topmost branch. All six feet four of him was stretched out from a teetering ladder that was held more or less firmly in place by a small crowd of happy Navajos at the bottom. As a final touch Paul, who never under any circumstances loses his dignity, even when taking his noon-hour nap in a wheelbarrow, threw cellophane icicles onto the branches. I had shown him how but he apparently considered my system too wildly abandoned. He would stand off, study the tree carefully for a minute or two, take one firm step forward and slowly toss one small handful at the spot he had decided upon.

For the next ten days, until we took it down, occasional Navajos could be seen trudging up the hill to hang a glittering can lid or a shiny candy wrapper or a pretty stone on their Christmas tree. At night it was the only light in all the desert around. I think the Navajos must have felt delight when peeping from their hogan doors to see it glitter on the horizon. From the road to the north it could be seen from a long way off. But from the south, no one traveling at night could see it until he came around the turn just above the post. Then there it was, in all its color and sparkling brilliance, framed between masses of pinyon and juniper.

In a dark corner of the storeroom I had a box tucked away into which, all year long, I had tossed bits of ribbon, artificial flowers, junk jewelry, and anything else that might please the souls of small Navajos. A friend with a chain of ten-cent stores always sent us off-season toys that would have cluttered his storage space. So, at Christmas time at Wide Ruins, Halloween masks, Fourth of July sparklers, and cherry-decorated hatchets would appear. Every year the number of Christmas stockings I filled grew larger. I could well believe that the population of the Navajo tribe was increasing by leaps and bounds.

The stockings came in the whole range of children's sizes, from babies on up. Into the toe of one I would stuff its mate and then fill the leg with toys, fruit, and candy. Babies would get a can of Gerber's, but they probably wouldn't like it. I fought a losing battle trying to persuade the Indian mothers to feed their infants baby food instead of fry-bread, coffee, and undiluted canned milk, the basis of the Navajo diet. Even at a nickel each, the Gerber cans on the store shelves went untouched.

The stockings made an almost impenetrable fringe along each store shelf, and the storekeepers had a maddening time of it for the one day that the stockings hung there unclaimed. Then, on the date that our home-made posters had announced, Navajos arrived by truck, wagon, horseback, and on foot. Each child chose a stocking of the right size and the shelves got back to normal.

As an extra inducement to persuade a family to send its children to school, there were special stockings for schoolchildren hung on the storeroom door, labeled with each student's name. One year little Lafe Terry, who was only five years old but who was so persistent in his wish to learn that the teachers let him sit in on classes, thought that there was nothing for him. He couldn't see over the counter and his stocking was hung low. Big tears rolled silently down his cheeks until Hosteen Glish noticed him. My husband Bill, in his role as Santa Claus, called out in an impressive voice "Lafe Terry" and hastily handed his stocking over. A big smile suddenly appeared behind the tears, and Lafe clutched his overloaded stocking to his chest, wrapping both his arms around it to keep it from dragging on the floor.

For the grown-ups there was an endless supply of coffee, doughnuts, and popcorn balls. Mrs. Beaver usually got the news of the party late. She nearly always arrived late for everything. But now she could be seen walking down the road at a clip faster than at any other time of year. She had her youngest child by one hand and the poor toddler flew through the air at every third step, being hauled along by his mother's firm grip. She strode, panting, into the post and thrust the child toward us and the remaining stockings. Having accomplished her part of the mission she sat down beamingly on the loafers' bench by the stove while the baby tried unsuccessfully to hide behind her skirts. With much coaxing by me and much threatening by Mrs. Beaver, small fry was persuaded to come breathlessly forward for a stocking. Clutching it precariously, he wandered back to mama, faintly murmuring "Clismuss."

We gave wool shirts to Paul and to Hosteen Glish. Hosteen was impressed by the paper that his was wrapped in, red and white stripes broken by madly dashing coaches-and-fours. Hosteen earnestly studied the pictures, then finally his brow cleared. He pointed triumphantly with a stubby finger and announced in tones that implied that he had successfully solved a most difficult problem, "Sinapasch!" an Indiana wagon.

To Chester we gave a handsome calendar all decorated with pictures of horses. Jimmy Toddy got a box of candy and a tooled belt. Patsy Martin went off beaming and loaded down with presents. The Cousinses had give her a couple of things. She also had the week's supply of funny papers which I always saved for her, two stockings full of things for her children, a large salt shaker, and some old socks that she had fished out of our waste basket. My Christmas present to her weighed her down even more. I had given her ten yards of velveteen so that she could make blouses for her whole family and have some left over for the medicine man who was going to perform a sing over her sheep. The sheep had been bewitched by Blue Red Man so a sing was absolutely necessary.

Early in December we put out bright wrapping paper and ribbon for sale in the trading post. This innovation was a huge success. I thought the customers must have been papering their hogan walls, but the packages that they brought to us were prettily wrapped and tied. Paul Jones did not wait for us to open up his gift. He told us that it was a saddle blanket that his wife had made.

Lukaichukai's wife, the oldest one, came in, her feet in cozy warm galoshes. She presented us with a turquoise ring and made a long speech in such rapid Navajo that all we caught was that we had been friends of Lukaichukai and that Lukaichukai had been friends of ours and that this ring was for us. Two weeks before Christmas she had told us about the ring, had trudged in through snow in weather that was only ten degrees above zero and was raw and miserable besides. She was on foot and had come four miles in broken shoes and a threadbare coat that had obviously come from some missionary barrel. It was splendidly buttoned with two tremendous Navajo silver buttons and, in between them, one black bone one. She had no gloves so I gave her a pair of mittens that I had knitted and an old pair of stadium boots that I had been saving for just such an occasion.

It always took a long time on the day of the Christmas party for the crowd inside the store and the bundled-up crowd outside in the snow to dwindle away. But at long last there would be no guests left and off in the distance the riding chant would be confusingly mingled with school children's voices: "Bingle bells! Bingle bells! Bingle alla hay!"

_____

_____

_____

_____

NINE

Joe and Jimmy Toddy

The Toddy family lived three-quarters of a mile south of the trading post. We knew that three-quarters of a mile was the exact distance because we measured it. Joe and his three children, Mary, Faye and Jimmy, had a hogan on the west side of the dirt road and Little Woman, Joe's mother, had a thrown-together hogan on the east side. Little Woman's home looked like an untidy pile of brush but inside it was neat and clean and comfortable. In the last years of our stay on the Navajo Reservation Jimmy had built himself a rectangular three-room plastered house. Travelers looking for the Wide Ruins Trading Post often mistook his house for the post. So we measured the distance and erected an informative sign that urged them onward. Although Jimmy had lived in that spot all of his life the 3/4 fraction proved a psychological hazard. He arrived at the store one afternoon in a state of complete exhaustion, explaining that he had walked all

Faye, Joe, and Jimmy Toddy

the way from his house, as he had done hundreds of times over the years. I expressed surprise that such a short hike had worn him out. "Short?" he indignantly replied. "It's three or four miles. It says so on the sign you put up!!"

We hired Joe Toddy as our handyman. In the winter he tended the fireplaces in all the rooms, shoveled snow, fed the horses, and saddled them when they were needed. He also generally made himself useful in the store. In the summer he raked leaves, swept the walks, and watered the flowers, as well as caring for the horses. His son Jimmy usually came to work with him, and Jimmy more and more because a part of our lives. He is still a part of mine, coming to Santa Fe every couple of months accompanied by a large bevy of children, all of whom call me Grandma. Jimmy's mother had died before we knew the Toddy family, and Jimmy long ago adopted me and began calling me "Sallie-Mom," as he does to this day.

Recently a letter from one of Jimmy's children, a second-grader, informed me and instructed me, "I will write you again grandma so don't worry that I well [sic] not. Please be careful and take care of yourself. Take your vitamins and stay out of the cold."

One year when Jimmy was a little boy, my husband's mother came to spend Thanksgiving at Wide Ruins and stayed on for a few weeks afterwards. It was the time of the year for the magnificent ceremony of the Shalako at Zuni Pueblo, forty miles south of Gallup. Wearing their eight-foot-high masked costumes, the six Shalako performers and their attendants come into the village from the nearby mountains. They cross the shallow Zuni River and dance all night long in six high-ceilinged houses especially prepared for them and their blessings. Bill's mother was anxious to see this event, which we had often told her about. When we loaded up the car for the trip Jimmy happened to be sitting on the bench in the store. He had been tracking a squirrel over by the corral but the squirrel had taken refuge in a

Toddy family in front of Little Woman's hogan. Photo by Bob Branstead

woodpile, so Jimmy had come in for a while to warm up by the store stove. On the spur of the moment we asked him if he would like to go with us. Though he only grinned and ducked his head, he was sitting beside me in the back seat as we drove to the pueblo.

The next day, when we stopped in Gallup to attend to business at the wholesale houses, Bill's mother went to Woolworth's and bought a drawing pad, some watercolors, and a box of crayons. She gave them to Jimmy when we got home. Several days later Jimmy returned the pad, a painting or a drawing on each page. To us this was the first indication that he had unusual artistic abilities, although the teacher at the Wide Ruins school had already recognized his talent.

In a quiet corner of a storeroom we built young Jimmy a desk. We kept him supplied with paints and paper, but he didn't always approve of our choice of paper and would often rummage through the wastebaskets to retrieve wedding invitations, stationery of pretty colors, or any other sheets that appealed to him. Working in his corner three or four days a week, he produced hundreds of pictures over the years. We arranged exhibits in various parts of the United States, and these exhibits nearly always sold out. We kept the prices very low and all the money went directly to Jimmy with the exception of the occasional gallery percentage. As he grew older the prices increased. Under the name of Beatien Yazz, he is now a well-recognized Indian artist as are several of his sons and daughters.

Jimmy saved the money from the sale of his paintings until he had enough to buy a dun-colored horse which he named Sliver [sic] after hearing The Lone Ranger on the radio. The Ranger owned a magnificent horse named Silver and Jimmy's Sliver did not resemble it very closely. But Jimmy loved Sliver and was proud of it. He often rode it to the post and kept it in our corral until it was time to go home. He was always good with animals. When his small dog broke its leg he constructed an ingenious contraption that fitted across the dog's back and held the splinted leg off the ground. He now has a pet chicken named McNugget.

A house guest one summer, a sun-loving artist from California, wandered the hills around Wide Ruins wearing only trousers and a hat. The Navajos dubbed him No Shirt. When Jimmy began to paint, also in trousers and hat, he was naturally called Little No Shirt, even though he wore a shirt. In Navajo that is Beah Etin Yazz so I printed that translation for Jimmy to sign his work. He carefully studied the letters but did not find their arrangement to his liking, so he rearranged them slightly to spell out Beatin Yazz, the name he still signs to his paintings.

In his early teens, Jimmy and his good friend Sammy Davis went off together to the Bureau of Indian Affairs boarding school in Riverside, California. There they honed their knowledge of English, surely one of the most difficult languages to be learned by someone who grows up speaking another tongue. Jimmy already knew much more English than I ever learned Navajo but at that time his writing style

Mary Toddy. Portrait by Peter Blos (No Shirt)

was still rudimentary. Soon after they left Wide Ruins a reassuring letter arrived, "We came in alright. We didn't get in mixed up." Other letters soon followed, "Everything are all in good Order. The grass are getting turn green here. At also the trees are getting to turn green. Here are planting flowers and crop already. I plant a flower for my teacher some time ago. When we went to town I saw everythings. I mean not everyone. Just a few of them. I saw the big mountains. I am the same as you are. Glad about all."

Joe Toddy decided to keep Mary and Faye closer to home and entered them as boarders in the Catholic school at Saint Micheales near Window Rock. Faye, a gentle, quiet girl, soon adjusted to the school routine but Mary, always rebellious, ran away one night. The next morning there was a phone call for Joe on the trading post line. Joe was suspicious of the strange instrument that we talked into and I had to bolster his courage while he stood three feet back from the box and gingerly held the receiver a foot away from his ear. In the end I had to take the message about Mary's disappearance and relate it to Joe.

Frighteningly, Mary was gone for many days. Joe called upon a local star-reader to find her. Certain men are blessed with the ability to gaze at the star-lit dome above them and to see events transpiring in other parts of the world. They can narrow their observations down to specific places or people. Thus Mary was discovered to be staying with a family in a hogan on the mountain between Saint Michaels and Wide Ruins. She was brought home and spent the rest of the school year helping her grandmother and cooking for her father.

In the spring Faye and Jimmy came home, too, and the united family prepared for Mary's Kinalda, the puberty ceremony during which the girl becomes the essence of Changing Woman, one of the most beloved and powerful of the supernatural beings. To assure an abundance of material goods in her future life, I loaned several necklaces and bracelets for Mary to wear while she knelt at a stone metate and ground enough meal to fill a deep pit that had been lined with corn husks under a layer of soil. A fire, built on top and kept burning all night, cooked the dough into a cake that was shared by the attending crowd. Mary was then stretched out face down on a pile of blankets that had been temporarily donated by the many guests while a well-respected older woman of the community pressed and molded her young body so that she would grow straight and strong. As some chants from the Blessing Way were sung Mary ran several hundred yards to the east and back again, her loosened hair streaming in the early morning breeze.

While visiting my sister in Colorado Springs, Bill and I bought two horses from a nearby ranch. Back at Wide Ruins we hitched a horse trailer to our pickup truck and started north to bring the horses home. Joe Toddy went along to take care of them on the trip back. This was a momentous trip for Joe. He was to be exposed to many things that he had never seen or heard of before. He wore a brilliant orange rayon shirt, a beaded buckskin vest, and a new black sombrero. As a final elegant touch he had bought one of those ten-cent bottles of perfume and dumped the entire contents over himself. As it was winter when we made the trip we could not keep the car windows open, so all the way to the Springs we gagged and choked while Joe sat proudly beside us.

When we arrived at the Broadmoor Hotel in Colorado Springs, Joe followed us hesitantly into a tiny room off the rather austere reception area. When the room began to move upward Joe turned pale, and he was downright terrified when the doors opened on the elegant mezzanine. We reassured him but he didn't quite believe us until he tested the floor of the new scene with an exploring toe.

Joe had brought along a bow and some arrows to defend himself and the horses when he camped beside them at night on our way back to Arizona. Defend them he did when he woke to find two men untying the halter ropes. The would-be horse thieves must have had

Joe Toddy at the Broadmoor Hotel

a frightening surprise when an arrow whizzed by them. The next morning Joe couldn't have been prouder than if he had won an Olympic gold medal. "They run fast," he said, "they real scared of me." The bow and arrows had nearly gotten him into trouble early one morning at the Broadmoor. He was found sneaking from bush to bush on the golf course, his bow at the ready as he stalked two deer that were strolling across a green.

We visited the Cheyenne Mountain Zoo and were given a special tour of the closed area where the animals from warm climates are kept in the winter. We had to keep close watch on Joe to prevent him

Joe Toddy and me with an orangutan at the Cheyenne Mountain Zoo

from wandering too close to the unguarded bars of the cages where tigers and other dangerous animals lived. I suppose that it was because they were so big that he wasn't even aware of the elephants until an exploring trunk swept past his chest. With that he was out the door and part way down the mountain before we would lure him back. He came willingly when he discovered that he was to be allowed to take an orangutan for a walk. Joe had many stories to tell his friends at Wide Ruins upon our return.

World War II disrupted all our lives. Bill was called into the Navy. For months I commuted between Wide Ruins and San Diego. Joe went to work in the roundhouse in Winslow and then in the mines at Morenci, and Jimmy joined the Marines.

Jimmy was in training at Camp Pendleton. Because Bill was a commander in the Navy, his request for Jimmy to spend his time off with us in San Diego was readily granted. The officer in charge of Jimmy's group reported that Jimmy was a crack shot in target practice, as were several of the other Navajos. "But," said the officer, almost in tears, "I can't get them to clean up the grounds when it is their turn and I can't make them do it."

Jimmy was trained as a code talker. This group of Navajos completely baffled the Japanese in the South Pacific by the use of a code based on the Navajo language. But the war ended before Jimmy could use his training, and he went to northern China with the occupation forces instead. A letter from Tientsin in 1946 said, "As this evening I'll answer back to your nice successful letter. Which I received yesterday. The thing are pretty good around here, the weather is too much changeable—mostly every day. There isn't nothing going on Around here in Tientsin. Such as that we are going to work in every day. And sometime we going on liberty. have lots of fun And that all is the news about Tientsin." On his return to Arizona he stated firmly, "I'm going to do more sketch or paint instead of loaf."

Not long after Jimmy came back, his father also returned, but only for a day. I think Joe intended to persuade Jimmy to part with some of the money he got at discharge. But Jimmy's guardian spirit must have been keeping a sharp lookout, for Jimmy had left on some mysterious mission of his own two days before. Joe strutted into the store smoking a large redolent cigar and looking most important and pleased with himself. He was wearing the same orange shirt that he had bought new to wear to Colorado Springs, the same black sombrero. He told a wild and woolly tale about having to kill an Apache down at McNary where he had been working in a sawmill. "Shoot 'em before he kill me."

TEN

Witchcraft

Some aspects of human thought are universal. Witchcraft, whether by that name or another, seems to be a notion all mankind holds in common to a greater or lesser degree. With the Navajo, it was, and probably still is, an ever-present force in human affairs. Because they know that the white man takes a scornful attitude (honest or feigned) toward the belief in overt wizardry, Navajos do not readily admit to white people their own convictions that such powers do exist. Occasionally, however, during our time among them, the subject would come up. When it did, I was fascinated, and I would later write down what I had heard.

Ben was a non-Indian friend of ours who had grown up in a remote part of the Navajo Reservation with only Navajo children to play with. He thought like a Navajo and had trouble living between two cultures, the Anglo that was his heritage and the Navajo that surrounded him during his formative years.

As an adult he took a job as a range rider in a part of the Navajo country where he was a stranger to the people whose livestock used the range he supervised. This was during the period of stock reduction, which the Navajo stockmen fought bitterly with every means they could command.

At Pinyon, where Ben was range rider, lived a medicine man named Gani Choii who admitted to having the supernatural powers of a witch. In the Southwest, among those who do take witchcraft seriously, it has been the custom to use the term witch to refer either to a man or a woman. Gani put those powers to work to combat stock reduction and naturally focused on Ben, the local embodiment of that hated program. Gani chose to hex Ben by a method called Praying Him into the Ground whereby an evil chant accompanied by some witchcraft paraphernalia was directed at the victim's head and progressed down his body to his feet.

Ben came out of his house one morning and was horrified to see an indication of the hexing pointed at his door. Other government workers would not have recognized it for what it was but Ben's Navajo-trained reflexes recognized it immediately. In a bad frame of mind he mounted his horse which, perhaps detecting his upset state, threw him into an arroyo, thus proving that the hex was taking immediate effect. A series of small accidents confirmed Ben's fears. He quit his job and moved off the reservation to a small ranch south of Gallup where he thought he might be able to escape the hex. But it apparently followed him there and culminated in the loss of a foot, which he shot off when he was cleaning his gun.

That spring we met him in Gallup. He joined us in lobby of El Navajo, limping in on crutches. He was thin and his face was drawn. His eyes looked truly haunted. A few months later we were saddened but not surprised to learn that Ben had died.

I have a necklace. Small whole shells, bits and pieces of larger shells, turquoise, and stone discs compose the double strand. At the bottom is a crescent made of material from a car's battery case and inlaid with a mosaic of turquoise. A few inches above the crescent on either side are two animal fetishes, one white and one dull red, which must have come from a prehistoric ruin. The necklace had belonged to Crip Chee, a notorious character at Wide Ruins who became a good friend of ours in spite of his reputation. There was something winning about the old scamp. His practical jokes were always so ridiculous, his two loud words in English, "Well, hello!" so brash that he brightened up our days for us and we laughed with him. We heard that his behavior had irritated and angered other traders and that then Crip would turn mean and perhaps dangerous. He was rumored to be a witch, and perhaps there was some truth to that accusation. Late one night, coming home from Gallup, we topped a small hill and

Crip Chee and the Lippincotts. Photo by Ray Pinney

suddenly had a swift, frightening glimpse of what now seems an apparition but most definitely was not. In the glare of our headlights rode Crip Chee, bareback on a running horse. He was nude except for a breech clout and his long gray hair was streaming behind him, unfettered by the usual head band. As Navajos' fear of skin walkers and other evils which are abroad only after dark keeps them safely holed up in their hogans at night, this was an unexpected sight indeed. Was old Crip one of those evils?

Hosteen Yazzi was also supposed to have evil magical powers. Ada Shorty was on her way to the trading post one day when her nose began to bleed. She sat down on the edge of the wash until the bleeding stopped and then went on to the post. When she came back the blood that had dripped onto the sand had disappeared. She hunted around and found that the bloody sand had been gathered up and taken onto the hill where it had been covered with pinyon twigs and needles. She was frightened and ran home. Two days later she became very sick. Her body felt as if it were being pricked with pine needles. She grew worse and worse, and finally she told her family what she thought was the cause. Her father called in a medicine man who read the stars and saw a vision in which Hosteen Yazzi was gathering up the blood and casting spells upon Ada by evil chants. Hosteen Yazzi was accused to his face, but he denied any knowledge of the affair. Then the medicine man held a powerful sing directed against Hosteen Yazzi and Ada got well.

Margaret Holt claimed that Lukaichukai was a witch. We weren't very surprised at the accusation since any Navajo who stood out from his fellows in any way might be accused of being a witch or wizard. That was one of the reasons why it was difficult for a Navajo to become a leader. As soon as he stepped ahead, the rest of his people no longer respected him but actually believed great evil of him. So no one could have much money, much personal prestige, much recognized ability in any way and still be accepted by the group.

Lukaichukai

Margaret hadn't much reason to think Lukaichukai was a witch. He was a wise old man from anybody's point of view. He was a medicine man who knew many of the intricate ceremonies and chants and therefore had real power. Power can be turned to good or evil. So he must have been the target of fear and envy many times. Margaret only said that when Harold Clark was chanting a healing ceremony over a young girl, he looked up and saw Lukaichukai and the girl died. That must have seemed rather far-fetched even to Margaret because she switched off onto other witches that she really knew more about.

Red Man had hexed Margaret's sheep. Certain Navajo men and women are gifted with the power to diagnose the cause of illness or other troubles by a technique known as hand-trembling. They think themselves into a trance during which their hands and sometimes their whole bodies shake and tremble. Their hands gather the solution to the trouble and relay it to the brain or to the mouth along with the identity of the correct cure. Margaret was a hand-trembler and used her gift to diagnose the reason for her sheep dying. Her shaking hand should have told her that it was because she didn't watch her flock carefully enough; a ram with a wildly roving eye had mixed in with the ewes for a week or so before being chased away. The result was that lambing time came way ahead of season and many of the sheep died. But Margaret's hand had other ideas. It led her to the center of the sheep corral and there it dug a hole, and down in the hole was some witchcraft paraphernalia. I wasn't told just what it was. A medicine man was called in, and he read the stars and saw that Red Man was the villain. So the next spring Margaret had a sing to cure her sheep of the hex. Hex or sex, I hoped her sheep would pull through all right the following winter.

Maybe it was because of jealousy that Red Man had witched the sheep. Or so Margaret thought. Or maybe it was because of jealousy that Margaret's hand accused Red Man. Before leaving Wide Ruins when the war broke out we had bought both Red Man and the Holts a flock of sheep each. Maybe the Holts and Red Man's family had worked themselves up into a tizzy of competition over their sheep.

Margaret took a direct part in an affair that had to do with the bewitching of her sister, Katherine Kee, so the story of that incident was more detailed and complete. Tom John wanted to marry Katherine Kee. Katherine was reluctant because Tom John already had two wives (a not uncommon situation at the time), neither of whom were particular friends of Katherine. Tom John pleaded, demanded, and finally threatened Katherine. He told her that if she didn't marry him she would be sorry. A vague threat to say the least, and maybe Tom John only meant that he could offer her more than other Navajos since he had more sheep, more horses, and more credit at the trading posts than anyone else around there.

But three days later Katherine got sick, then sicker and sicker. Finally, Margaret was called in to do hand-trembling to diagnose the cause of the sickness. Margaret's hand led her over the wash, up the hill, and in among the trees to a tchindi hogan. "You know we don't ever go to those places where someone has died," she said, "and a baby died in there." Yet Margaret went into the hogan and over to the place where the baby had died. In confusion at what I thought was a contradiction I said, "But you went in. Why did you do it?" "My hand took me in," I was scornfully told. "Why naturally," I scolded myself, "what a dumb question." In humble, and rather horrified silence I listened to the rest of her story. Whether or not the baby was buried where Margaret dug I don't know, and I don't know that I want to know. But after the earth had been pushed aside she found some rags and some strands of hair. Apparently her hand then ceased leading an independent life and its supernatural powers deserted her, leaving her in the lurch. She got out of that tchindi hogan as fast as she could and made a beeline for home where she told what she had found. Again, a medicine man was called in to read the stars. This time his vision was pretty complete. It was summer and Katherine Kee had been sleeping out in the open under the pinyons and junipers. One night, along came Tom John, sneaking from tree to tree until he was within reaching distance of Katherine's head. He rummaged in his pocket, pulled out a knife, and snipped off some of Katherine's long hair. He took so little that when Katherine woke up she didn't know she had lost anything. But Tom John made spells over the hairs, and it was he who had buried them in the most dreadful place he could think of. When Katherine's father heard this story he climbed on his horse and went galloping off to John Joe's hogan. He told Tom John what Margaret and the medicine man had discovered, but Tom John denied the story. Atsenni yelled at him and said that if his daughter died he would kill Tom John. John tried to soothe Atsenni and told him not to worry, that Katherine would be all right in a few days. "Sure enough," said Margaret triumphantly, "in three days she begin to get better and pretty soon she well." When the stars were read again, this time all the medicine man saw was a small cloud of black hair blowing away in a soft soft wind.

ELEVEN

After the War

As it did for everyone all over the world, World War II changed our lives drastically. The United States was not yet involved in the war that was raging in Europe. But Bill had been in the ROTC at the University of California, so he was an officer in the Naval Reserve. A passing truck driver delivered his notice to report for duty. It had been sitting in the Chambers post office for several days, so Bill had to leave immediately to meet the deadline that he was given. He was assigned to harbor defense school in San Francisco and then transferred to the San Diego Naval Base.

I made occasional trips to La Jolla, where Bill had rented an apartment. But I also spent much time at Wide Ruins. One Sunday morning I was idly toying with the radio at the post and, the one and only time I have used that switch, turned on the short wave. I got the bombing of Pearl Harbor!

When it seemed that the war would be all but endless we sold Wide Ruins. Bill and Jean Cousins went to Los Angeles to do their part in a war factory there. I moved to the San Diego area until Bill was sent to the South Pacific. Then I bought a small house in Berkeley so that when Bill did come back, he would have a home to come to.

The man to whom we sold the trading post was not popular with the Indians so he lost customers and could not keep up his payments to us. At the end of the war we bought it back from him. I wrote Bill and Jean, asking them if they would like to lease the post until we could come back again. Jean said that Bill knocked over all the furniture getting to the door to send me a telegram saying that he wanted to go back to Wide Ruins under any arrangement we wanted to establish. He was tired of civilization; everything went too fast, everyone drove like fiends, there was too much racket, and there were too many people.

When he went back, all the Indians who had taken their trade elsewhere came flocking back bringing friends and relatives with them. Business was booming and keeping Bill busy. My husband went down there on a hurry-up trip right after he was discharged from the navy and reported that Bill was running things in his own individually ethical style. Rationing was still on, and Bill was imposing his own rationing system on the customers. With supplies limited he was doling out short items to those who, in his estimation, really needed them. Those who didn't need them didn't get any, even though they had the stamps entitling them to a share. "If I let everybody have some," he explained, "everybody gets just a little bit and nobody's satisfied. This way some of them are mad at me but the others get as much as they need and at least they are happy."

I wouldn't be surprised if Joe Martin were one of the Navajos who profited most by Bill's informal method of rationing. We had a soft spot in our hearts for Joe and his family. He used to work for us until we found that he had a very contagious form of T.B. and then we regretfully had to let him go. Tuberculosis, of one kind or another, was a very common and serious ailment on the reservation. Joe was honest and gentle, with a sense of the ridiculous that was aimed at himself as much as at anyone else. His customary friendly helpfulness gave poignancy to the bitter tragedies that too frequently overtook him. Because neither Joe nor his wife, Patsy, believed in the hygienic practices preached to them by the doctors from the mission hospital, their children sickened with tuberculosis and died one by one until only the eldest, Rose, was left. We once spent a sad day at the mission hospital where they had decided desperately, but too late, to take their boy, Mountain, after the medicine man had failed to cure him of tubercular meningitis. Never again would we listen to anyone who says that Navajos are unfeeling and unemotional.

Joe was constantly moving to new hogans in hopes that the spirit

Joe Martin

of evil would thus be evaded. But soon the drying up of his cornfield, the death of another child, or the stampeding of his sheep were proof that the evil had only moved with him.

One summer day, Patsy and Rose Martin were out herding their sheep. They had two children with them whom Henry Chee had asked Patsy to mind for him that day. Henry himself was going off to a sing that was being given to help a friend ward off a snake bite that he was convinced would happen to him sometime in the near future. In the middle of the day Patsy suddenly remembered that she had intended to make herself a new skirt to wear to the last day of that same sing. The last day and night is the time when the grand finale comes to all sings. Then the most colorful ceremonies are danced, the most mysterious magic performed, and the greatest crowds are gathered. Patsy had not yet been to the trading post to use up the last of the credit she had earned for a rug. She intended to buy ten yards of print percale for a new skirt, and she wanted that skirt for the sing. So she told Rose to watch the sheep, and to take care of the small child and toddler, and off she rode to the post.

She did her bit of trading with more than usual dispatch. Even so it took her at least an hour and a half to decide between a serviceable multi-colored stripe and a dashing but impractical flowered lavender print. With the serviceable stripe finally under her arm and her last note of credit due torn up and thrust into the store stove, she rocked off on her bony horse to rejoin Rose. But within half an hour she was back at the trading post. The horse was lathered and Patsy was in a panic. Not long after she had left Rose and the sheep, two coyotes had gotten into the flock with the idea of carrying off some of the young lambs. Rose had sternly commanded the smallest Chee child to stay right where he was and she had taken the other by the hand and started off to chase away the coyotes. She rounded up the frightened sheep and went back to the juniper tree where they had all been sitting. The child was gone.

Rose, Joe, and Patsy Martin

At that moment Patsy rode up and she and Rose searched together for the little boy. But it was late in the day and Patsy was afraid that night would come and the child would not yet be found. So off she went to enlist the help of Bill Cousins. She knew that Bill would not fall for any cooked-up hard-luck tale. But she knew equally well that he would be the first to metaphorically come galloping to the rescue if he knew someone was really in trouble. Sure enough, as soon as Bill heard her story he organized an efficient search party. Patsy led the group as she had the best eyes and could see the best to track. She followed the baby's erratic footprints slowly, for it was hard to detect such small disturbances of the dry, rocky soil. They had been looking behind every clump of rabbit brush, under every tree, and into every gully for about three-quarters of an hour when along came Henry Chee on his favorite pinto horse. He had been lolling around his hogan all day and was just then getting off to the sing. He himself was sporting three shell necklaces and a massive silver belt and his

horse was done up to match in a silver-decorated bridle. For added
dash there was a rope neatly and impressively coiled over the saddle
horn. All in all, Henry was feeling swaggeringly pleased with himself.
Bill never did like Henry and liken him even less when he was in this
mood. Henry announced that there was no use looking further for
the boy, as the child had wandered into his hogan safe and sound a
half an hour before. Then he rode up close to Patsy, glared down at
her, and demanded to know just exactly whey she had let the baby
get out of her sight. Bill felt that there was some justice in this scold-
ing, but he didn't like Henry much so his sympathies were all with
Patsy. Still and all, it wasn't any of his business, so he just stood by
and listened. Henry's language became more and more abusive, and
finally Bill decided he couldn't stick around without getting angry, so
he went back to the trading post.

The next morning Joe came in to buy two big bottles of Sloan's
liniment, some Mercurochrome, and a roll of adhesive tape. "You
setting up a hospital?" asked Bill Cousins. "No," said Joe sadly. The

Patsy Martin

medicine was for Patsy. After Bill had left, Henry Chee had become more and more angry and had finally uncoiled his rope and severely beaten Patsy with it until she was badly cut and bruised. Then, his temper having had its fling, Henry rode off to enjoy the rest of the night at the sing. No doubt he stood in the chorus and helped cure his friend's potential snake bite.

When Bill asked Joe why he hadn't taken a hand to protect his wife, Joe offered what to the mind of any Navajo would be strong reason indeed: Henry and Patsy belonged to the same clan. Henry's sociological relationship to Patsy was stronger than Joe's own. He could not intervene without violating this strong tradition.

Apparently Bill Cousins understood Joe's resigned attitude, but he certainly didn't feel any resignation himself. As he told the tale he unfolded his long length from its usual negligent pose against the counter. He began to get angry all over again at the memory. "I told Hosteen Glish to take the afternoon off from being handyman here and to go to that sing," Bill said belligerently, "and to tell that Henry Chee to come in here, that I wanted to talk to him." Bill's sense of chivalry had beaten down his usual policy of noninterference with Navajo ways. "Henry came in the next afternoon to see what I wanted and I gave that no good four-eared coyote a dressing down. Who did he think he was, whipping Patsy that way?" That long-tailed bobcat! He's just like all that Chee outfit. A bunch of bums. Why the blankety blank so and so! I oughta . . . Hey, Hosteen Glish! Go tell Henry Chee I want to see him again."

We were back. Nothing had changed much. Some of the old people were gone, and there were some new babies. The children and the trees were taller and the gullies a little deeper. But each individual grown-up Navajo seemed just the same age as he had been five years before when the world went to war. The Navajos did seem glad to see us—even the rapscallions of the community, which makes me wonder whether we should be proud or embarrassed. Black Rock came into the trading post and, although he was so old that each year must have made a tremendous difference to him, he looked just as handsome, just as dignified, and just as kind and wise as he did when we left. Pretty Boy was still as cross-eyed and as bashful as ever, his hair still ragged. He looked like a character out of A Midsummer Night's Dream. Another boy who was really beautiful, whom we called The Little Shepherd, was dead. He had been killed while working on the railroad during the war. We missed him. He was so good to look at although we never made any progress at all towards being friends with him. He was as beautiful as a Donatello statue, lithe and quick. But he took fright at any interest directed toward him and fled. Once Joe Toddy astounded me. He asked, "Some men say there are wild men. Is that right?" I took a quick contemplative look at Joe with his long hair bound down with a purple band, with hunks of turquoise tied with bits of string through holes in his dusky ears, and I told Joe that there were people who were called wild. I said that perhaps the Little Shepherd might be called wild. Joe thought that over solemnly and agreed. Then I said that I would very much like sometime to get a picture of the boy. Joe relayed the information. The Little Shepherd ran out of the store door and off over the hill and did not come back for months.

Lukaichukai, too, had died. During one wartime winter he had given a sing for a sick Navajo down toward the railroad and he had ridden back home through a snowstorm in the middle of the night. He was so old. Even a young man might not have stood that twenty-mile trip. Lukaichukai had been a captive of Kit Carson when the U.S. Army finally subdued the Navajos. He must have been more than a small child even then; when the Long Walk was over and the tribe was back in its homeland, Lukaichukai was made a tribal policeman. It was only recently that we had learned that he used to come

Black Rock. Portrait by Peter Blos

down from the mountain whenever he heard that we were home from the coast. Although he spoke no English at all and we spoke only the little Navajo necessary to get along in the store, Lukaichukai must have felt the same kinship with us that we felt with him. I hope he did. I would feel very proud to know that he looked upon us with favor. He was a true medicine man, dignified and with the wisdom of ages in the wrinkles of his face. We missed him very much.

We also missed Joe Martin. Poor Joe. He was stalked by tragedy until the very end. He died of the tuberculosis that had killed his babies one by one. His newest hogan did him no more good in escaping the evil than had any of the previous ones.

Joe Toddy was gone, but only temporarily. He was living high, wide, and handsome up at Canyon de Chelly with one of the local unattached women. I was pretty sure that when Joe learned that we were at Wide Ruins he would come back and apply for his old job of handyman. Bill Cousins said that he had had a letter from Joe some time earlier. It said that if his son Jimmy had any money or war bonds

Joe Toddy and Lukaichukai

around the post to send them on to Joe immediately. Bill said Joe didn't write very well, and he wasn't sure he deciphered the message correctly. And anyway Bill just didn't think he'd be able to get around to sending Joe the bonds that Jimmy had left locked up in our safe.

Joe Toddy kept himself pretty well in hand while he was working for us because he seemed rather afraid of the two Bills. They were both tall and Joe was short. Whenever he got out of line at all, they would call him into the store and leave him in the center of the space before the counter. Then they stepped up on the slight elevation behind the counter, glared down at him sternly, and took turns berating poor Joe for whatever he had done. After such a session Joe was a wilted man. Then for weeks afterward he would be almost too good; he radiated goodness until the brightness of it almost wilted us.

Not only did Joe get in trouble with the store management occasionally, but he also got into trouble with the other Navajos. His troubles with them usually followed a pattern that had all the likely-looking young women in the neighborhood woven into it.

When Jane first came to work for us as a housemaid we foresaw difficulties, as she was unusually pretty and had a great deal of gay young charm. Poor Joe. He was called up before the post counter by the two Bills one afternoon. He came in nervous but with a certain bravado because he knew he hadn't done anything at all this time that could possibly be wrong. He hadn't taken so much as a safety pin from the store or a flower from the patio or a slice of bread from the kitchen. He hadn't tracked mud into the living room and he had remembered to keep the ashes shoveled out of the fireplaces. Ever since that last awful lecture when Bill Cousins had told him that he had to mend his ways and Bill Lippincott had fixed him with a fearsome eye and shouted, "Joe Toddy!" he had been very careful to walk the straight and narrow path. He had heard that a new maid, a pretty girl, was coming to live at the trading post, and he must have had one or two fleeting thoughts about the possibilities the situation might offer. But he hadn't even whispered a word of his thoughts to anyone at all. So when both Bills threatened him with dreadful fates if he should so much as look cross-eyed at the new maid, Joe was convinced that these white men had read his mind or else that there was some sort of witchcraft mixed up in the affair. In either case there was no doubt left as to his awful punishment if he should have any more thoughts in Jane's direction. The law had been laid down and Joe, by jingo, followed it.

There was one morning when the whole store was full of Indians mumbling interestedly about why Joe still hadn't turned up for work. It seems that he was being stalked across the desert by an irate father who had been warning Joe to cast his sheep's eyes at somebody else's daughter. But Joe, always weak about such matters, had been caught at dawn that morning out in the sagebrush with that same daughter.

To complicate matters, another daughter was there too. Papa had fired a gun at Joe but missed twice, and by the time he got set for a third try Joe had disappeared into the nearest canyon. How the whole thing was finally settled I never did find out, but Joe turned up late in the morning very much the worse for wear, and everybody seemed to be mad at him. Even our housemaid Jane angrily flipped a dust rag around the living room and spat out, "That Joe!!" Then her dusting became more thoughtful and she finally giggled. "A man chased my sister once," she confided, "She hit nose with fist."

The Navajo woman is not the submissive, sweet Indian Maid of the Waters of Minnetonka School of Thought. The Navajo woman stands up for her rights. The Hogan is hers, the fields are his, and remain his until fall brings the harvest. Then, once in the hogan, the produce is hers. While the family sheep are all herded together, usually watched over by the women or the children, each sheep is owned by an individual and is kept or disposed of only by that individual. A wife can divorce a man simply by setting his possessions outside the hogan door.

Reading on the screened porch one afternoon, I heard a commotion on the other side of the garden wall. I peeked out the little window that opened on to the courtyard of the store and there was an interesting commotion indeed. Harry Tso was running round and round, ricocheting off first the garden wall then the wall of the store, and then, being shunted off from the one open side by a bunch of laughing Navajos, bouncing off the wall of the hay barn, only to make the rounds again. His wife, Gloria, pursued him wielding a long-handled shovel and shouted firmly at every step or two, "I'm just a poor helpless woman!!!" Whap! "A poor weak woman!!!" WHAM!!! Whatever Harry had done, I am sure he never did it again.

Elsie and Sadie, two young Navajo women who worked for me one summer, came back the following year to help dip their mother's sheep. I told them they could spend the night in their old rooms. They said it was the first good night's sleep they had had since they left our house. I guessed that was true as the next morning, long after dawn, the proper time for Navajos to be up and around, their mother came charging through the kitchen, up the stairs, and, in two minutes flat, Elsie and Sadie came scurrying down rubbing their eyes and looking abashed.

After a while, John Lee took Joe Toddy's place as handy man. At first we hired Little Shorty but he began to work slower and slower and finally went AWOL for four days. His job wasn't waiting for him when he got back. He consoled himself by painting pictures in an old notebook that we had thrown away and that he had retrieved. He built himself a small foot-high table, Jimmy Toddy gave him some poster paints, and, sitting flat on the hogan floor with his legs stretched straight out under the table, he set earnestly to work. The paintings were fascinatingly primitive and imaginative. (They are now at the Laboratory of Anthropology in Santa Fe.) There was no

Little Shorty's family

Crip Chee in his chariot

perspective and no shading. The arrangement of the elements was almost geometrical and the elements seem to have no relationship to one another. One of the pictures that I like best has a hogan at the top. Conventionally enough, the hogan is built of brown logs; but the roof is chartreuse. Down in the lower left-hand quadrant of the paper is a bristly blue squirrel with a red mane. In the right-hand corner are a cooking fire and a pot.

Crip Chee hadn't changed one iota from the same mischievous old devil who had once tried to hide a whole crate of oranges under his coat and get out the door without us seeing him. His knowledge of English was still limited to a loud "Well, hello" with a hearty pumping handshake. Crip had sawed his wagon in two, thus transforming it into a chariot pulled smartly by his team of one large bay horse and one small brown donkey.

The Cousines temporarily lived in a tent up on top of the hill until they could get moved into their own house again from ours. At five o'clock one morning Crip Chee walked into their tent and woke them by breathing a loud "Humph!" The he sternly demanded to know what in the world they were living up there for. Bill Cousins said that if he had had a gun there would have been a repetition of the time that an earlier Wide Ruins trader took a shot at Crip!

Even the ants were the same. I couldn't understand it. There were still big anthills in exactly the same places where they were five years and more before. The ants were as busy as ever but the hills stayed the same size. I came down from the horse corral to get the key to the tack room and there, trudging up the path, was a bunch of big red ants carrying a yellow paper match. Then when I got down into the patio there was a bunch of little black ants lugging off a cigarette butt.

Three weeks earlier we had moved out of our house in Berkeley and started our furniture Arizonaward in a moving van. It still hadn't arrived. We were living in a state of suspension. I managed to round up a saucepan or two that we had left there, six assorted plates, three cups, and two dozen glasses. There were some jelly glasses and cheese glasses, too, but I had put them out on the hill to turn purple. The desert sun does that to cheap glassware. I had tried to get a whole set of glasses purpled that way once before. I got too discouraged to try again. I had set them out for about a year in a corner of one of the ruin rooms, and they were just beginning to turn. While we were away on a trip the daughter of a white woman working for us came to visit her. Lulu prowled around, dug up a few walls of the prehistoric ruins that surround the post, carved her name on a handy cliff, and generally took an interest in the country. She ran across my cache of glasses and took them triumphantly home with her as an example of ancient tableware. This time I hid these new glasses behind a big clump of sagebrush.

Jimmy Toddy came back along with a truckload of melons. He had written me from San Diego that he was getting out of the Marines Friday and "P.S. Don't answer back it." He got as far as Winslow by train and there the melon truck picked him up. His sea bag had arrived two days earlier, horribly adorned by a gruesome picture of a wounded Marine.

Jimmy began to paint again. We turned Bill's old office up on the hill over to him and all day I agonized over what sort of pictures he would produce after his wartime experience. Some carpenters went up in the middle of the afternoon to move some bookshelves out of Bill's old office and into the new. I went up there more to see what Jimmy was painting than to see how the carpenters were getting along. I was sure that we would have to steer him away from battle scenes or pin-up pictures. As I should have known, it didn't do me a bit of good to go up. Just as he used to do when he was little, as soon as his domain was invaded he folded up his pad of paper so that no one could see what he was drawing. Then he himself went and stood in a corner as far away from everyone else as he could get. That afternoon he wasn't frightened as he used to be. He simply didn't want to be disturbed.

I confess that later I sneaked up to his little house on the hill. I couldn't stand the suspense. Again I might have known. Instead of a grisly painting of a Marine in the midst of battle, there was a picture of a soft gray deer stepping over a fallen log.

Just as we had hoped, his term with the Marines seemed to have done him a lot of good. Somehow all the toughness and unpleasantness passed him by. He was gentle, kind, thoughtful, and much more self-assured than he had ever been before. But he was still quietly bashful, too.

I had had an interesting letter from Jimmy written on February 21, 1946. "Hi there. Also I'm station here in Tientsin China. We just come in here a couple weeks ago from San Diego. We have been sailing accrossing for 20 days, we got in here in North China and our weather is too much changeable mostly every day. And there are three Navajo boys are they come with me from San Diego. But those three boys are they are not with me up her in Tientsin. They are station in somewhere in Russia across the broader, I think. That's what I heard sometime ago. But they are lots of them they with me up here in Tientsen." So he was not alone although the Navajos who were with him were not people he had known before. He was longing to be home again in Navajo country. In the same letter he wrote, "What are going on around Wide Ruins. Say will you tell me about it. P.S. Answer soon. Please."

Back home, in his studio on the hill Jimmy did a particularly well-composed painting of two eagles attacking two small fawns which were looking up with frightened eyes. A doe and an antlered buck were charging the eagles to drive them away. It was a good picture full of action and interest. As I carried it in through the store to put it away with the rest of the paintings, I noticed that only Jimmy's cousin Philip Shorty and the Mifflin were in to trade. I didn't think that Jimmy would mind having them see the picture even though ordinarily it would embarrass him to have it put on display to the Navajos. I waxed most enthusiastic. Turning to Jimmy's cousin I said, "This is really a fine picture. Jimmy did good work. Have you seen it?" When Philip nodded yes I still raved on. I turned to the Mifflin and asked him if he had seen it. The Mifflin simply stared. Again I said, "It's a good picture, Mifflin. I like it. You haven't seen it. Do you want to look at it?" The Mifflin stared for a minute at the rolled up painting and then back at me again. "No," he said in a final and definite tone.

The Mifflin was a mysterious child who inexplicably appeared one day at the age of three, tied in back of Jimmy's grandmother, Little Woman, as she rode her bony old horse down the hill to the store. From that day on they were always together. When I asked Jimmy who the child was he replied airily, "Oh, he's a mifflin." The mystery was never resolved.

The store was closed on Sunday. But one Sunday morning Ned Striker came to the door of the house crying and asking for help. His brother had died the night before and Ned needed new clothes to bury him in and a blanket to wrap him in. Bill was busy in his darkroom so I took Ned through the house and into the locked-up store. Together we chose new pants and a new shirt, a pair of shoes and a soft blanket. If I had opened the store door to let Ned in, Indians would have appeared from nowhere wanting to trade and I would have had trouble closing up again.

Ned was distraught but I did not realize until later just how distraught. For several months he had been wooing Charlie Mack's wife, who showed no interest in the wooing and, in fact, was finally so

The Mifflin

annoyed by Ned that there was a meeting of her clan elders to resolve the situation. Charlie and his wife were completely satisfied and happy in their marriage so Ned had been given orders to stay away.

The day after Milton's death, Ned, perhaps under the influence of some cheap wine as well as the emotional upheaval of losing his brother so unexpectedly, had, against the dictates of the elders, stumbled over the hills to Charlie's hogan.

Charlie's oldest daughter, age eleven, was out on the mesa with the sheep. She came home with her charges that evening to find the hogan door locked and no answer to her calls. As she reported to a group of Navajos in a hogan in the next valley, she had peeked through a crack and saw her mother and father asleep on the floor. Her little sister was sitting on a blanket crying and did not respond to Aggie's questions.

Sensing trouble, the entire alerted group of Indians followed Aggie back and broke in the locked door. Much to their horror they found Charlie and his wife, not asleep but dead, their heads bashed in with a tire wrench that lay near the bodies. Little Mary on her blanket was alive but with a terrible head wound and torn eye. But she was conscious and told of an attack by Ned Striker. She identified him without a doubt.

The dreadful news, of course, came immediately to the trading post, the central point of the neighborhood. Luckily two missionaries from the Ganado Mission happened to be in the store and they immediately took charge of the two little girls. Mary was taken to the hospital where an operation to remove splinters from her brain was unsuccessful. Three weeks later little Mary died. Aggie was taken in by her clan relatives.

Ned was now a marked man and he realized it. Trying to outthink him, the two Bills went to Isaac Shorty's place where he had collected several old cars. They removed all the spark plugs so that if Ned tried to steal a car, he would not be able to find one that would run. But instead of a car he had stolen a horse, and his tracks were plainly visible heading toward the highway.

Bill Cousins knew somehow that Ned had pawned a concha belt at a trading post in Holbrook so he telephoned there and suggested that perhaps Ned might stop in to redeem his belt before going into hiding or before trying to leave the country. Then he and my husband joined the group of outraged Navajos who were expertly tracking the stolen horse.

I was left armed with a rifle to patrol the store and house, the buildings Ned had wandered through such a short time before. Every time I passed the telephone I tried to reach the police at Window Rock. But night came and I still got no answer.

I didn't know which way Ned was heading, but there was a possibility that he would circle around and try to raid the store for money and goods. Suddenly I heard something at the laundry door. I thought Ned was trying to break into the house. I had never before been able to understand how anyone could take part in a lynching. When I remembered what he had done to that fine Navajo family, particularly to the little girl he had left alive, I was actually hoping for a chance to shoot him. Fortunately the noise was only a dog at the garbage cans.

The men on Ned's trail had borrowed some horses themselves. They were so expert at their job that they arrived at the highway to find Ned's horse still lathered and to learn that Ned had boarded a westbound bus just fifteen minutes before they arrived. Early the next morning Ned walked into the Holbrook trading post and presented the pawn tag for his belt. The trader's wife was alone but when she was the name on the tag she coolly said that the belt was locked in the pawn safe and that she would have to phone her husband to come and unlock the safe. Then she went to the phone and called the sheriff. Ned was sentenced to serve two life terms and was still to be tried for the death of the child.

Epilogue

We left Wide Ruins in 1950. The years of World War II had brought changes to the lives of all Americans. The Navajos were no exception. Many of them had left the reservation to join the services or to take war-related jobs. They saw other cultures and the fabric of their own lives was torn.

Changes were afoot all over the reservation. The Tribal Council was coming under the domination of a man from Washington and of a strange little Russian. He was, confusingly, born in Georgia, Russia and had lived in Moscow, Idaho. Under their domination, rules and regulations were passed that were insupportable for the traders. The United Traders Association met in Gallup again and again and finally hired Ralph Carr, the former governor of Colorado, to represent them at a hearing before the Congressional Committee on Indian Affairs. Bill and other traders appeared to testify. The situation was more or less resolved, but it left a bad taste in everyone's mouths.

Bill became increasingly restless. He had always wanted to have either a cattle ranch or a boat, so during the war, when we thought that we had already sold Wide Ruins, we bought ranch land in Oregon. When we repossessed the trading post and moved back there we often took time off to drive to the ranch. We were building a house there, doing the building ourselves after clearing an acre of land in the surrounding forest.

When we made a trip north we would take a truckload of our possessions with us since by that time we knew we would leave Arizona permanently. On one of the last trips we took the horses. I cried when Paul Jones reached through the slats of the truck bed, patted the horses' hooves, and whispered a good-bye.

That trip was not a good one. We took a shortcut through the Black Rock Desert in Nevada that turned out to be the proverbial shortcut—the kind that makes you wish you had gone the long way around. The Black Rock Desert was a large expanse of desert country with no signs of civilization other than the dirt road we were on. As night came on we looked for a place to camp. We knew that the horses were tired after a long day of traveling. Then, off in the distance ahead of us, we saw the twinkling of a campfire. Never having seen anyone in that stretch of country before we drove on out of curiosity. Suddenly a man staggered out of the bushes and fell into the road. With screeching brakes we stopped, leapt out, and converged on the blood-covered figure. Two days before, during which no one came along, he had turned his jeep upside down in an arroyo. He managed to crawl out and to get a fire going during intermittent spells of consciousness. Surprisingly he was wearing a sailor's uniform. Bill, to keep it clean, was wearing his Navy commander's cap. We put the poor man between us on the front seat, looked at our road map and saw that the nearest town was just across the state border in Oregon. Telling the tired horses that we were sorry, we headed for Oregon. I held the man upright. During periods of consciousness he would try to tell us what had happened, then would glance at Bill's cap and add a respectful "sir ."To our dismay, when we reached the spot on the map that we were headed for, it turned out to be nothing but a filling station and three houses. We turned south and drove for hours to Winnemucca where we left our passenger in the emergency room of a hospital.

We sold the post to the Navajo Tribe. We had better offers but we did not want any trader to have a monopoly on the posts in that part of the reservation. While hiring outsiders to manage the store the tribe would still keep control.

The weekend before we left Wide Ruins for good, the Navajos, at a great gathering near the post, asked us each to talk to them. It was a difficult good-bye. But on the final day, when the dogs were loaded into the station wagon that I was driving and the last load of furniture was in the truck that Bill was driving, I was glad to be on our way. The new managers had moved in the day before. Prices in the store were immediately raised. In contrast to our simple furnishings, be-ruffled lamps and doodads from National Park curio stores were placed around the rooms of the house. I did not want to see more of what was going to happen to the place and the people who had meant so much to me.

Months later I cried again when a laboriously written letter arrived from Hosteen Glish asking us to come back and enclosing five dollars to help pay our expenses.

One of our last acts at the post was to bundle up the store books, the wool book, the pawn book and the daybook, the ones that Crip Chee had so delightedly shoplifted, and, at John Adair's request, send them off to the Cornell University Library. John and his wife and small son had spent many weeks with us while he was writing his book on Navajo and Pueblo silversmiths. He had done his research at Pine Springs before we took it over. The people at Pine Springs have always been known for their jewelry, particularly so-called sand-cast silver. (The silver is not cast in sand in spite of the nomenclature. The mold is cut into soft volcanic tuff.)

Now that I am living in Santa Fe, Indians from Wide Ruins occasionally come to see me. Most of them now have pickups or vans. One night not long ago, after I had gone to bed, the dogs began to bark. I went out to see what was disturbing them, and there in the road stood six Navajos from the trading post. Unacculturated Navajos do not knock, because only Evil knocks. So there they stood just hoping to be noticed. I was very glad to see them. They were on their way from Wide Ruins to Durango, Colorado, where one of the family was at school. They had decided to stop off to see me en route, a detour of only a few hundred miles. They stayed all night, slept all over the house, and ate everything that I had in the refrigerator. The next morning I had to go out for breakfast.

It saddens me that several years ago the Wide Ruins post was completely destroyed by fire. Jimmy Toddy phoned me from Chambers to tell me the news. I understand that the site has been bulldozed. But it still exists in my memory and I often reconstruct it in my dreams.

Index